COMING FULL CIRCLE:

Paradise Lost…

Paradise Found

By

JIM ARNOLD, M.D., ret.

Copyright March, 2004

Jim Arnold

Mar. 28, 2805

Edited by: Susan Schofield
Publication Preparation and encouragement by: Jennifer Owen

LCCN: 2004099527

ISBN: 0-9766959-0-1

Printed in the United States by Morris Publishing
3212 East Highway 30
Kearney, NE 68847
1-800-650-7888

DEDICATION

This book would not have been written, nor my journey so awesome, if it had not been for my wife and best friend, Pattie Boothe Arnold. The steadfastness inspired by her Cherokee Indian blood, patience and stability have kept me alive and inspired me to be who I am. Without her, my physical life would have ended some time ago. I can only say, "Thank you, Pattie. I love you."

FOREWARD

As an astrological consultant, it has been my privilege for many decades to have joined with others in their personal life journeys. And while my clients have generously shared with me their trials and tribulations, their triumphs and successes, it is clear that the ability to navigate easily through the waters of life is a significant challenge for most individuals.

When faced with severe hardship, lack and limitation, the natural response for most of us is to react with anger, bitterness and resentment. This is even more so the case when the challenges of life are overwhelming and become too hard to bear.

We become frustrated, irritated and begin to believe that life is simply unfair. If our seeming problems worsen, we often finally decide to give up on the whole thing. Yet we all know, in the deepest recesses of our hearts, that there is another way, a higher way to respond to the events of life.

In *Coming Full Circle,* Jim Arnold shares with us his personal life story and the many ordeals presented to him along his walk through life.

What I find most remarkable about his telling is that, while he probably had every reason to respond with bitterness and resentment, he managed to find another way to define his life, and to live it from a new and awakened perspective.

Many civilizations tell the story of a mythological "fire bird" that burns itself in the flames, then is reborn from the ashes beginning a new cycle of life. Known in some cultures as the Phoenix, this amazing creature is associated with triumph over adversity, and is a symbol of transformation, resurrection and spiritual rebirth.

The Phoenix became a favorite symbol on early Christian tombstones, and was associated with the resurrection of the faithful and the rising above the sufferings of life.

i

Jim's book is a reminder, and a living example, that no matter in what fire we might find ourselves, it is possible for each of us to experience a rebirth to a new and wonderful life.

As he so clearly relates in his story,

I suppose there are several titles one could give to this experience. It is the reason for writing this book - to show that no matter who one is, where one is, or what one's environment is, self-love can be attained.

What a powerful statement this is! For without the love of self, how could we possibly learn to love God and our neighbor? As Jim repeatedly points out, there is no separation anyway between God, you and your next door neighbor.

The lessons in this book strike at the core of the human dilemma. And what is even more impacting is that Jim, through his own life story, has shown us that there is indeed another way to live life, and it is truly magnificent.

Thank you, Jim Arnold, for sharing your story, your music and your self with the rest of us.

Jim Hays
www.jimhays.com

ACKNOWLEDGEMENTS

I never expected to write a book, didn't know how and didn't think I had anything to say. Still may not. As my awakening continued after one magic episode at the Esalen Institute on Big Sur, in California, it was impossible for me not to share my joy of life with any that would listen and were ready or at that place in life where a part of them wanted something other than what they had found in the Earth life.

As I began to share, sometimes without even using my voice, it became obvious that a few liked what they saw and/or heard. This was brought obviously to my attention when the wife of my own family physician made an appointment to see me in my Radiology office. She told me that she had noticed a remarkable change in me over the past year and I radiated a different energy, one of joy. She asked if I could get that for her husband. He was my most dear and trusted physician, the best whom I have ever known.

So, even though personal changes had not been so obvious to me, those who mirrored me spoke otherwise. Unfortunately, personality change is not something that can be packaged and meted out.

Finally, after many had listened to my ravings and said "You need to write a book," the final confirmation came from my Editor-Astrologer Jim Hays, who constantly re-enforced that opinion. His invaluable suggestions and guidance will not be forgotten. While the reader may find this to be another boring biography, I have to say these things so you will understand the rhythm of my journey.

Those who had the most influence on me will be mentioned, some more than once, in the body of the book. This Earth journey of mine could not have been what it was without the particular family of which I chose to be a part. It may seem to the reader that I am complaining about my family, begrudging the fact that I was born in this specific environment. That is really not so. I love them all deeply, even though the ones yet living may not understand that. The things of which I speak had to be in order to make this book real, believable and not just another boring biography, although some may find it so.

While the book seems to be all about me, it is intended to be about you, the reader who I hope will find something in it that will help you discover your own innate worth and beauty. I cannot tell the story of another's life, only my own.

My wife Pattie and my sons, Bruce and Kevin, have all been a grand part of this journey and had to survive it so that I could get to where I am. I hope that the reader finds this to be a survivor's manual and realizes that the life preserver is within each of us.

TABLE OF CONTENTS

FOREWARD I

ACKNOWLEDGEMENTS III

TABLE OF CONTENTS... V

1.CONSIDER THE CIRCLE.. 1

2. A BETTER WAY 3

3. FINDING MY LIFE'S PURPOSE....................................11

4. BUILDING A LIFE..19

5. LOOKING INSIDE 23

6. THE RE-CREATION 25

7. THE BIG BANG 31

8. DISCOVERING THE DRUM...................................55

9. LEARNING TO LOVE 59

10. THE LESSONS CONTINUE 71

11. MOMENTS OF HAPPINESS 91

12. JOY OF THE DRUM 95

13. THE DRUMS SPEAK 99

14. WHAT I BELIEVE 117

15. FURTHER REFLECTIONS....................................125

16. COMING FULL CIRCLE 141

EPILOGUE..145

CONSIDER THE CIRCLE

Where does it start? Where does it end? There must be a beginning and an ending, mustn't there? I have always been taught that all things begin and that all things end. Surely it is written in stone somewhere. Could it be I was taught an untruth? Could it be you were too? Even modern science is beginning to think that the Universe didn't start, and that it will never end. What a concept – what a revelation! It just is!

Consider the circle, a universal symbol of wholeness and completion. Like science's new vision of the Universe, it too has no beginning and no ending. Therefore, ponder this: If we are all travelers on the Great Circle called Life, as the title of this book suggests, then perhaps our journey also has no beginning or ending. If we have never left this Great Circle, maybe all we have to do is remember where and what we have always been.

My own story has no real beginning or ending. Your life story is the same, whether you recognize it or not. Eventually, all of us will come to understand this and finally realize the stories we are living will never end. They will go on forever, just like the circle.

The circle also represents feminine energy. Perhaps this is why I named the book as I did, signifying the balancing of the yin and yang, the female and the male energy. In my opinion, this is the ideal merging of the energies.

Even though I tell my friends that I had my left brain removed so that I could just "feel" and "know," there is still a bit left. Now, using this bit of reason and if logic prevails, I must have started somewhere on this Great Circle. Since one point is as good as another, I must choose a moment in time to begin my story. And staying true to the circle, I must come back to that point at the end of this account.

I know. Let's pick a place on the arc of the circle where I nervously knock on the door and enter trembling into the office of my new psychotherapist. The fact that my therapist was a woman was not an insignificant fact at that time in my life. Could the male energy inside me accept what I was about to blurt out while fighting back tears?

A BETTER WAY

"I don't want to hear any of this crap about hating my mother!" Little did I know at the time how that statement would come back to haunt me. Here I was, in a psychotherapist's office not really knowing why I was there. I just knew that I didn't want to die.

A few days earlier, I had attempted suicide by aiming my car at a bridge embankment by putting the pedal to the metal. At the last moment, the thought came to me that there had to be a better way than this. Fortunately, the meeting between the bridge and my car never took place. And while I managed to avoid ending my outer physical life that day, inwardly I was still living in utter despair and in desperate need of help, whether I was able to admit it consciously or not.

I was in my early fifties, Chief Radiologist at a very fine hospital, with all the exterior signs of success or at least successful as most of the world thinks. My wife Pattie was quite stable, my age, and had stayed with me for several decades. Thinking back on it, I am amazed that she did not leave me. For in those anticipated final moments of self-destruction, my world was totally negative. No matter where I looked, I could find no inner or outer loveliness. I could see nothing of any value or worth. All I could behold in my vision was shame, loneliness and a dreadful fear of living. In short, my life was a total mess. In order to understand how I arrived at this most miserable state, it is necessary for us to go back on the Great Circle to my early childhood and to those events through which I lived.

As I stated in the dedication, this book would not have been written, nor my journey have been so awesome, if it had not been for my wife and best friend, Pattie Boothe Arnold. It has been her patience and stability that have kept me alive and inspired me to be who I am today. There are no words that can even begin to describe the gratitude I have for her presence in my life, and for the touchstone that she is to me.

Our connection goes all the way back to the late 1920's, and our early childhood in Cordell, Oklahoma. Since we are the same age and grew up in the same small farming community, one might think there would be some similarities in how life there influenced us. As I discovered over the years there were none at all. We might as well have been raised in different countries. Although we went through grade school and high school together, I was not even aware of Pattie except at those times when our parents tried to get us together. She played basketball, but I was not a sports person. Well, in total truth, I was not a person at all. I was what I thought my parents wanted me to be. Pattie, on the other hand, always seemed to know who she was.

I remember distinctly an incident while attending a county basketball tournament. Pattie was a guard, had the ball, and was dribbling down the court at full steam with a most determined look on her face. I could see her clearly because I was at the Cordell end of the court, standing beneath the basket. My thought at that time was, "I sure wouldn't want to go out with her." It's strange how things turn out.

There was another reason why I did not particularly like her. She was just too smart, always at the top of the class, and voted outstanding senior girl. And there I was, third in the class, following behind my fellow classmate Dan Fisher, who was considered even more reclusive than I.

On one occasion, I even had to give Dan's salutatory speech because of his shyness. Of course, it followed Pattie's valedictory speech, which only made things worse from my perspective. I had no idea at the time how much our own perception creates the reality we experience. From my viewpoint, all this suffering was being piled onto me from the outside by a harsh and unjust world. It just wasn't fair!

At one time, I was considered for the outstanding senior boy award, but the committee felt that the individual needed to be a sports person to hold that honor. I definitely was not into sports, and the committee passed me over. That cut me to the quick, and helped to further solidify my feelings of unworthiness.

4

In our school, students had to go out for sports, or take band or glee club. I don't know what possessed me, but I went out for basketball. The odd thing was is that I really didn't want to. As I reflect on it today, I suppose I just wanted to be what a boy was supposed to be. I tried sports and it did not work for me.

The ongoing search to prove my lack of worth was even present in our first basketball practice session. Out on the court we divided into teams. Our side got the ball, and one of my team members passed it to me. I didn't want it, and quickly passed it to another team player. In spite of my best efforts, my teammates kept throwing the basketball to me. That was just too much responsibility!

As I ran down the court, my stomach kept bouncing up to my Adam's apple, and that was not a good thing. I simply was not going to be accountable for the outcome of any game, and my level of stress went through the roof.

It is really sad to think how we adults can crush our children's spirit with our limited definitions of what they should or should not be. As for me, I know that was certainly the case growing up in high school. Try as I might, I could never seem to fill the role I was called upon to play.

I was uncomfortable in the locker room because I was not circumcised as most boys my age were, but I managed to conceal that. I did not ask myself at the time why this was so important, but I did feel it. It meant I was different and unloved by my parents, since all the other parents had done this for their boys, as my parents had done for my older brother.

I was searching, as I did almost all of my life, for proof that I was unworthy and unloved. It became an obsession for me and prepared me well for a life as a self-destructive workaholic. It was also one of the main reasons I considered ending it all at the bridge embankment later in life.

Soon after that, a boon came my way in the form of a heart murmur. Someone, a school nurse perhaps, heard a murmur and sent me to the local physician, who then sent me to a Cardiologist in Oklahoma City. He could find no real reason for the murmur, but suspected it might be secondary to a mild, unrecognized case of rheumatic fever from early childhood.

As he finished his examination, he made a statement that puzzles me to this day, although it served my purpose at the time. "Jimmy should not go out for sports, but can mow the yard and things like that." Now, that might mean nothing to the modern reader, but when I was in high school, there were no power mowers. We had to use heavy old steel mowers that took a great deal of energy to push, even with a frequently mowed yard. I remember how exhausted I would be after mowing, and I was in fairly good physical condition. With the physician's recommendation, I was able to quit the basketball team, but I was still required to participate in some school activity, so I went to the choral room.

I hated band because the band instructor made me play the clarinet instead of letting me play the saxophone like my brother. I tried it, but had to fake playing because I did not learn to read music. I finally got out of that mess by taking a less noticeable seating in the band. I was satisfied to be the last chair in the clarinet section. Who was first chair? It was Pattie, of course.

Pattie and I were members of the same Baptist Church, and attended the same Sunday school. She was "saved" at an early age. I thought it would be wise for me to get "saved" also, and the opportunity came when the local preacher visited our Junior department and told us about hell. He came back to where I was sitting in the back row (you can't escape notice by sitting in the back row), and whispered in my ear that the only way out was by being "saved." I definitely wanted out, so it was the road of salvation for me.

From then on, I swallowed whatever was fed to me by zealous Christians and ministers, hook, line and sinker. I had finally gotten a belief system that would control me until I was 62 years old. But for Pattie, that did not happen. She patiently took only what seemed right for her and grew in stability and inner strength. She believed what she wanted to believe. Again, we were worlds apart, more than I could have ever known.

Even so, Fate seemed to bring Pattie and me together repeatedly while still in high school, but I was not aware of it until much later in life. As part of a school project, Mr. Street, the high school principal, had both of us print out maps of the school district. Part of our assignment was to do the layout for the lettering. We were both very good at printing, but as you might expect, Pattie was better.

Later on we were again brought together in an unforeseen way. This time it was in the school play, *Pecks Bad Boy*. I had a part in the play, and my best friend Bill Buie had also been cast for the performance. Pattie was to play his girlfriend.

I am still amazed that Bill and I would act in a play, since we were among the most shy of all the boys in school. I did not like to be in front of any group or class, but there I was playing Amy's boyfriend. I don't remember the girl who played Amy, but I do remember Pattie and the role she played. What do you think about that?

One of my lines in the play was to exuberantly exclaim, "I don't give a rap for Amy." While that seems very easy to say, it became a major problem for me as I could just hear myself saying, "I don't give a rape for Amy." And, of course, during practice, that is exactly what I did. My verbal blunder resulted in one of the most profound silences imaginable, followed by a huge burst of laughter from the group. I was mortified; sure they would think that I was really a bad person. As a child I had been told, and totally believed, "What a man thinketh in his heart, so is he." To me that could only mean one thing – I was a rapist. This was just more evidence of my poor self-esteem. No, total self-loathing would be more appropriate. The big night of the first performance came, and I was sweating blood. I knew the "best" citizens of Cordell would be in attendance, and all I could think about was how I was going to mess up my lines. I was sure my actor buddies were listening with great anticipation, hoping I would embarrass myself. But to everyone's amazement, including my own, I was able to deliver my lines correctly. Needless to say, the events of that evening are forever and indelibly written on my mind.

After graduating from high school, I went on to college at the University of Oklahoma. Pattie attended Oklahoma State University. I chose the University of Oklahoma because I was going to be a preacher and preach against "sin," therefore, I would have to go to a place where sin was practiced. And that place, in my mind, would be the infamous University of Oklahoma, OU.

Of course, God was leading me all this time, or so I thought. Having been taught to place all my troubles on Him (I believed God was male), it seemed only natural to carry this line of reasoning to its logical conclusion. I decided that since God managed to get me to OU, He was responsible for my grades. That meant I prayed more about it than I actually studied. And as absurd as it may sound now, at the time it made perfect sense.

By the end of the year, I found out that God was not very good at algebra, Greek or English Literature. He did barely get me by, but I began to think I would be better off attending a church school, like Oklahoma Baptist University. Whatever my reason for changing universities, it was a good decision. The personal attention of the new professors helped me understand my part in the learning process. Eventually, my grades improved.

Keeping busy with university activities, I didn't think about Pattie very often. I did not try to contact her, nor did she try to contact me. I was occupied with my studies and kept my social life to a minimum. Afraid of girls, I remained a virgin, and rebutted every advance that was made towards me.

One young student was particularly interested in me, but I kept my distance from her. Of course, I was terribly lonely and dreamed of having a date with a girl who truly cared about me. I was not willing to risk being turned down when asking for a date, because I wanted no painful rejections. So, I kept to myself, buried in my books and classes with an occasional foray playing the pin ball machine at the Wide

Awake Cafe. I ate most of my meals there and considered it my home away from home.

Another possible explanation for my lack of socialization was an unconscious fear I had of being accepted. If that happened, I would then be required to date, have other friends and take part in other activities. That was a responsibility I was not prepared to shoulder.

By the time I was a senior at OBU, Pattie had already graduated from OSU and was teaching at Tonkawa, Oklahoma. For reasons unknown to me at the time she began writing letters, telling about her teaching experiences and her love of kite flying. I did not respond to her invitation to come and fly kites however. To be honest, I didn't have the sense to know that she was romantically interested in me. With my poor self-image, I could not understand why anyone would want to share my company.

Eventually, Pattie managed to get me to accept an invitation. She got tickets to a Metropolitan Opera performance of *Aida*, which was being performed in Oklahoma City. We met there and enjoyed the magnificent performance with Blanche Thebom. From then on, our letter writing became more frequent, and we began spending time with each other. Pattie then moved back to Cordell, our home town, as Choral Director in the Cordell Schools. She was also Director of the choir at the First Baptist Church.

Our dating eventually blossomed into a full-blown romance, and for several years we were officially engaged. The engagement, however, came to a screeching halt when I revealed to Pattie that I had gone out with an old friend whose husband had recently been killed in an Air Force flying accident. While this was mainly for her support, I could not deny some feeling for her, again setting myself up to experience guilt. I asked Pattie for her forgiveness, and tried to explain my actions to her, but to no avail. Again I was searching for that person that would love me and was to find out later that I could not accept the love of anyone because I was not capable of loving myself. We broke up, and after some time, she went on to tie the knot with a local teacher. Pattie was

9

married in a Cordell church. On the day of the event, I was driving around the block which contained the church, wanting to dash in and yell, "Stop the wedding!" But, I did not. Years later I was to discover that Pattie had been hoping that I would do just that, make a scene, and interrupt the ceremony.

So, why didn't I, you might ask? I was already dying inside, so what difference would it make if I made a fool of myself in front of all those people who had seen little Jimmy Arnold grow up as a super nice boy? In my warped way of thinking, I was convinced that I had no right to obtain what I wanted if it might interfere with the life goals of another. I believed that the turmoil of my life was what I deserved, and it was almost a "sweet" feeling – a feeling of accomplishment, perhaps. Yes, I know. "Sick."

About a year later, Pattie got a divorce, and we began dating and re-established our connection. The fact that I was given a second chance to reconnect with her, and another opportunity to marry her, is something for which I will be eternally grateful.

3

FINDING MY LIFE'S PURPOSE

I had always admired the general medical practitioners in our hometown, and it appeared to be a calling worth considering. This became of extreme importance to me when I had the opportunity to attend the World Baptist Youth Congress in 1949, with twenty-one other Baptist Youth. It was a six week trip with two weeks spent on the MS Batory, a Polish Motorship, and four weeks spent touring Europe, culminating with a meeting in Stockholm, Sweden.

I was nineteen at the time, and recovering from an appendectomy. The operation had been done in a small town in Southwest Oklahoma in a very small country hospital. How well I remember the surgery! The doctor tried (I say tried because it did not work) a relatively new method of anesthesia. It was called a spinal block. I can still feel the deep aching pain as that stiletto was shoved into my back, and hear my groans as the procedure continued. Flipped over on my back a few minutes later, the doctor made his first shallow skin incision. I screamed since there was no anesthesia, and it was nice of them to stop and consider plan B.

In those days, ether was the preferred method of anesthesia. It was administered by dripping small droplets of the fluid onto a cloth mask over the patient's mouth and nose. I had already experienced the ghastly stuff while having a tonsillectomy as a child, but I was greatly relieved to breathe it in deeply in this instance. I would have done anything to escape the reality of the surgery.

The operation went well, but as is sometimes the case, the urinary bladder refused to empty on its own for a time. The common procedure, when that occurs, is to have nursing personnel pass a urinary catheter through the penis into the bladder for draining. Alas, there were no male nursing personnel, and I was in great stress from a distended bladder. The nurse brought in a catheter and tossed it to me. She looked right at me and said, "Do it yourself." "Wait a minute!" I thought, "Am I hearing correctly?" But, the pain of bladder distension soon fogged out the conversation and removed any reticence that I might have had to do this "evil" thing to myself. I actually did it, and the accompanying pain of passage of the "giant" catheter was welcome as the spillway of life was opened. Maybe I became a physician to "get even." No, I don't think so. The operation, painful as it was, did not prevent me from enjoying the European tour, but it did keep me from climbing the Matterhorn in Switzerland.

So even though I was "on the mend," I was looking forward to the trip to Europe, and was even anticipating meeting new people. The first person on the tour who got my attention was a beautiful young nursing student whom I shall call Kay. She was from Texas, and was studying at Baylor University.

I was strongly attracted to her, as was often the case in my earlier years, the old Arnold curse (personalized just for me) struck again. The thing that I wanted most was something that I did not deserve, or so I believed. This became a way of life for me, as you can see, but it was a way of life I determined for myself with my own limited outlook.

In my mind, I was not allowed to be happy since I had been born in this world to suffer, and was not worthy of being loved. So I attached myself to another nurse and became close to her, as a friend, throughout the trip. I fear I was more than a friend to her, so once again I managed to mess up someone else's life.

After returning home from the European tour, I wrote Kay, plighting my love, knowing that God had prepared for us a life of medical missionary work together. My belief that God had called me to medical service was why I changed from being a ministerial student to a pre-med student. It seemed only logical at the time, even though I never particularly liked the sight of blood and had never seen a naked woman, which I greatly feared.

I was so sure that Kay would accept my expressions of love that I had already decided to change my college major from religious education to pre-med. That meant taking a lot of science courses but I liked science anyway, except for chemistry. Chemistry was not only confusing, it was downright dangerous, at least the way I practiced it!

I sent in my application to the University Of Oklahoma School of Medicine, had a necessary live interview with the admissions board and waited. I was very honest during the interview, taking great pains to tell them that I was planning to be a medical missionary, although I had heard that the board frowned on those who were not going to stay in the state of Oklahoma and practice medicine. I didn't have to tell them that, so why did I, you might ask? As seems to be true of the workaholic mind set, which may be secondary to a severe case of poor self esteem, I was still trying to set myself up to fail, just like I had done many times before.

I had still not heard from Kay, but she eventually got back to me. She was kind enough not to send me a "Dear John" letter, and agreed to meet me for dinner at a restaurant in Waco, Texas. It was a long bus ride from Shawnee, Oklahoma to Waco, but the ride gave me time to "prepare" a spontaneous speech from my heart, ever changing, as I feared both acceptance and rejection. I must say, it was a fantastically gentle rejection that she delivered and made me love her even more, but I had to agree with her logic. She was engaged to marry a foreign missionary volunteer with hopes of serving in Africa. I let her know I was truly happy for her, and wished her a wonderful life. Eventually the two of them did marry, and they both served in Africa as missionaries. Ten years later she died from a brain tumor.

The desire to be a medical missionary stuck with me, and I felt it was God's way of finally getting me to where He wanted me to be. After all, what right did I have to make those decisions on my own?

If I were not accepted to medical school I could blame it on God and it would not be my fault. After all, I was planning on becoming a great medical missionary, the highest of all callings, I thought. Failing isn't so bad if it can be blamed on someone else, the subconscious told me. And to make this a little more hair raising (perhaps that is why I am bald), I had joined the US Navy Reserve when I first attended college at the University of Oklahoma, hoping we would go to war with Russia and I could get out of school. That was just the way I thought about things at the time.

When in high school during the Second World War, I would fantasize about being in the military and shooting "Japs." I had no concept of them possibly shooting back, even though they had killed my cousin who was aboard the USS Utah at Pearl Harbor. Those feelings have long passed. While I was waiting to hear from the medical school acceptance committee, I was called to active duty. Torture time! I had gotten myself into a fine kettle of fish. As one might have guessed, I did a whole bunch of praying because I no longer wanted to shoot anybody. I finally got my letter saying I was selected as an alternate for admittance into medical school. ALTERNATE! That just would not cut it. I called the Dean of Admissions, and told him of my plight. I must have been a good plight presenter because they did accept me. Fortunately, the US Navy was kind enough to put me on reserve status until I graduated from Medical School.

To say that Medical School was a unique experience would be an understatement. Even so, I managed to make my way successfully through all the required classes, reaching my final year of studies. At that time I decided to join the Navy's Senior Medical School program in order to receive a small monthly payment for my last year in school, actually, for the last nine months. I thought I needed the money and paid no attention to the small print which said I had to serve four years on active duty to pay it back. What was it Laurel and Hardy were famous for? Oh yeah, "Another fine mess you've gotten me into."

I graduated from Medical School and entered the Navy. During my first year in the service, I was put on one of the smallest warships going, a Destroyer Escort, and was sent to the South Pacific as Medical Officer for two of the small ships. I was quite proud when I checked aboard my first Naval Vessel. Walking up the ladder, I gave the Officer of the Deck

14

the snappy salute that I was taught to give, caught my toe on the top step, and went flying across in front of him, as my white hat rolled down the deck. His comment was, "Oh no! Another damn doctor." That was not to be the end of my discomfort that day as I had to check in with the Skipper, an old salt's term for Captain. His rank was Commander and mine was Lieutenant. He was quick to tell me that he didn't like Navy doctors because their rank was too high, and they made too much money. Welcome aboard Lt. James K. Arnold, USN! Yes, I had joined the "regular" Navy because I was convinced I would stay and make a career of it.

Except for the ever present "mal de mer" (sea sickness), it was great fun visiting the many small ports. I had the opportunity to see the Isle of Manus, Pango Pango, Australia, New Zealand, the Philippines, Hong Kong, Guam, Korea, and Taiwan Formosa, just to name a few. I did have problems with sea sickness though, and lived on canned fruit juice for two weeks until we got to Hawaii. When we docked I had just enough strength to get off the ship in the evening, go to a Hawaiian night club, get drunk (so I would have the guts to get back aboard ship) and had difficulty in doing so.

All this time, I had not forgotten Pattie. As we discussed, she had married a local teacher in Cordell. I still loved her. Was I acting out a TV Soap Opera or what? I had the occasional try at finding a girlfriend, but had resisted all sexual advances because I still believed that sex was to be saved for marriage.

Now, what I am about to tell you is against all that I learned as a sailor, as there was an unwritten rule that said "What happens overseas, stays overseas." If they want to come get this old man, then have at it. I tell this to "again" demonstrate how blocked I was as to the prospect of enjoying life. I made sure that was not going to happen. When we docked in Japan, I joined the Captain and three other officers and went to a local Geisha house. Of course, that is not true because real Geisha houses were of great repute while "our" house was of ill repute. They did serve a fine meal, however, and the Mamasan picked out an appropriate girl to join each of us while dining. It may be hard to believe, but I honestly did not have a clue as to what was going on. I really thought they were nice girls who were just being polite. I was raised to respect women, all women, and to me these young girls were no different. Ah, but they WERE different. They were well skilled in knowing when to ask their dining partner to go with them to the private rooms, and they left, two by two, until my "girl" and I were the only ones left. I refused to quit eating as I began to suspect that the situation was not what I thought it was. My eating mate kept asking me, imploring me to go with her. I must confess that I wanted to in the worst way, but just could not. Once again, my self-limiting beliefs were active in full force. I WAS NOT WORTHY OF THIS AND I HAD NO RIGHT TO DO IT. The poor girl got me so intoxicated that I could barely get on my feet and stumble from the place, trying to suppress deep sobs of despair. I was so angry with myself for not doing what the married guys were doing (yes, I was the only single one) that I tried to tear down the white picket fence in front of the house. Fortunately, I was not arrested and made it back to the ship, still trapped in my guilt system.

I am not telling this part of my life story because it is fun to tell. It actually hurts somewhat even to recall it. It does hit home, however, revealing why I had thought of life as I did, until the time of my "rebirth" in 1991. I was brought face to face with my worst fear and my greatest desire.

For me it was my worst fear because, in my mind, sex, or the absence of it, was what seemed to separate Christians from all others. To think that Jesus had sex, or even that his parents had sex, would be intolerable for many fundamentalist Christians. The Apostle Paul, if the story be true, was known for his supplication that it would be better if all were like him, and he evidently was not married.

How many times have I heard people say, "Not my parents!" when faced with the reality that they were an offspring of the sex act. In some of us, the belief is deeply ingrained that there must be something evil about the sex act. I am not talking about love. Sex and love are totally different, and I must agree with what "God" says in Vol. I of Neale

Walsch's *Conversations with God,* when asked, "What about sex?" The answer was, "Isn't it a great way to have fun!" I can just hear your mind dealing with this statement.

But, that is where I was. For the first time in my life, I was being given the opportunity to have sex, and with professionals no less! But as drunk as I was, there was still an overabundance of inhibition. The sex inhibition was so ingrained in me that I could not even have dreams of engaging in sex. The dichotomy or duality of the situation astounds me, but that is what makes this Earth life so intriguing, is it not? What had I been taught or had the perception of being taught as a child? It was none other than, "One has to have sex to be loved, but having sex is a sin."

I finally decided, following our next few weeks in patrolling the Straits of Formosa, that the sea, at least on small ships, did not agree with me. So I devised a brilliant plan in order to get off those rusty old buckets. I would volunteer to become a Flight Surgeon. Yeah, that was the ticket!

A few months later I was in Flight Surgeons School in Pensacola, Florida, still extremely lonely but very busy trying to fly a Navy airplane. Okay, get ready for this. You remember why I wanted off the ships, the throwing up thing? Well, my first flight with my Marine instructor in the overpowered trainer found me throwing up in my flight gloves. Trainees did not dare throw up on the airplane and I had forgotten to bring the "barf bag." I foolishly had to say "Yes" when the pilot asked me if it would be all right if he and another pilot, carrying another doctor, could do some dog fighting. Hell! I didn't know what that was, but I soon found out. I did finish the School but did not fly solo since my eyes kept me from qualifying to do that (thank goodness).

I didn't date while I was at Flight Surgeons School, and there seemed to be no good way to meet anyone. I did go to a few drive-in restaurants, and would fantasize about dating the waitresses, but never had the nerve to ask one. I would occasionally leave a very large tip and "run away" before they could thank me or ask what I really wanted (another symptom of my low self-worth). It was on one of those forays that I

17

found myself driving behind a young man whose girlfriend was sitting very close to him. Seeing the two of them together created such a feeling of loneliness and sadness in me that I remember thinking, "I wish I had someone to sit close to." Hey, we are talking about a grown man of twenty-eight here, at least chronologically!

I drove back to the base and went to my room. I immediately called Pattie, who was living in Norman, Oklahoma teaching choral music in the Moore school system, just a few miles from Norman. I asked her if she would like to get married, and she said yes. We made plans for her to fly from Oklahoma to Pensacola during her Thanksgiving break so we could get married. We did not invite anyone, even our parents. We felt we had hurt them enough but evidently they did not agree and drove together all the way from Oklahoma to attend the ceremony. The Naval Station's Captain came to our wedding also. How do you refuse a Captain? We were married by a Navy Chaplin and had a two night honeymoon in the Old Spanish Fort Motel in Mobile Bay. Pattie flew back to Oklahoma and we did not see each other for the next six months, as I was sent to the Naval Air Station in Denver, Colorado.

A few of you romantic souls may ask, "Why in the world did you do that?" Pattie and I have asked ourselves the same question many times as we laugh about it. No, she wasn't pregnant.

4

BUILDING A LIFE

Eventually, Pattie and I went on to build our lives. We had two boys, now middle-aged men. We are proud of them and did our best to raise them properly. We had heard from the various experts as to how one should raise a child, but I think most of them never had children. Believe me; it is much easier to give advice about raising a child, than to actually do it. However, we did the best we could with the abilities we had. And having been a parent, I understand what a challenge it is for most parents.

By the time the Eighties rolled around, one could say that our lifestyle was definitely good. There was money in the bank, a steady income and no foreseeable end to that. I had the start of a substantial pension plan and a flourishing career. There were even two properties other than the home in which we lived. By all modern definitions of success, I had "made it." But, as they also say, appearances can be deceiving. In spite of all the outward signs of achievement and fulfillment, my inner life was a black hole of emptiness, despair and self-loathing.

My "success" had turned into something else that almost brought about my demise. While I outwardly had no doubts about life, who I was and how life should be lived for me and everybody else, on the inside I was dwelling in a personal hell. I was living in a self-created prison of insecurity, self-doubt, self-hatred and the belief that I was doomed to fail at whatever I tried to do. These feelings were enforced by the failure of a business venture during which I trusted my accountant who held the controlling interest of the business. I began to awaken to her deceit when we were forced to declare bankruptcy and were sued by investors. I lost about $200,000 by the time it was over. I could not believe that I could have been so blind, but it did fit my personality to a tee.

Looking back on it, I can see now how I had always tried to do everything by the rules, especially while in the Navy. By following rules, I did not have to take responsibility nor did I have to think about choices. When the book said to inspect the ships to see if there were any health hazards, I left no bulkhead unturned, so to speak.

As stated before, the first group of ships to which I was assigned was Destroyers, larger than the Destroyer Escorts, out of San Diego. I had to make routine inspections of the galleys including the dishwashers which had a required minimum operating temperature. Captain Smith's galley had a defective dishwasher and, in my opinion, needed to be replaced. I could just see the local headlines, "Hundreds of sailors become deathly ill because the ship's doctor didn't keep the dishwasher hot enough." I really didn't see any problem replacing a dishwasher. The Captain thought otherwise, and unceremoniously removed me from his office. The battle cry had been sounded. I was going to see this through to the bitter end.

I immediately went "over his head" to the Flagship to talk to the Commodore of the Destroyer Division. The Commodore was very kind, listened to what I had to say, and we cordially parted. For some reason, I was away from the docks for several days after that and on returning was shocked to see Captain Smith's Destroyer in dry dock. When I asked why it was there, I was told it was because of me. The Commodore had come down on Smith like a ton of bricks and ordered him to replace the dishwasher. Wouldn't you know? To do that, the ship had to go into dry dock. Of course, Smith hated me from then on, and I tried not to see him again as I became too aware of the power of a military physician.

I was no different in my personal life than I was aboard ship – judgmental, critical, and afraid to make a mistake because it would prove to the world how awful I really was. This attitude carried over into the church and was perhaps the most harmful there, at least to me and my family. I would read nothing but medical and Baptist literature, thinking all other writings would corrupt me. I was even afraid to go into a Catholic Church because God would strike me dead. I was taught to think such hateful things about other denominations.

I tried to make up for not being a preacher or a missionary by teaching a Sunday school class, and by always being at the church whenever the doors were open. It exhausted my family, but my wife stayed by me and did not complain. I am fortunate she did not leave me. It was not surprising that our children learned to dislike the whole church environment, but that was also the only time they saw me. I was the workaholic father who was never at home; always more comfortable and in control at work.

I let a good friend talk me into becoming a Deacon in the church, although I did not want to be one. However my guilty feelings got me again and I agreed to take the position. It was not long until I found out that, like in many businesses, involvement in the church centered on power struggles, and was a way to control others and to have "importance" in the community. I am sure not all Deacons are like this, and many are honorable and God fearing men. My wife and I were proselytized by one large church, mainly for her experience in conducting hand bell choirs and my experience in tithing. I was so determined to do "what was right" that I considered not having a pension plan; an evil thing because it robbed God of money that should be His. I tithed so well that I was made vice chief of the Deacons of this large church, and followed the pastor around believing everything that he spat out.

It seemed that the more involved I became in the church, and the harder I worked at the office, the more depressed I became. You have to remember that my entire life up to this time had been lived with a fundamental sense of perceived worthlessness and total self-loathing. I saw myself as having little if any value as a human being; I was guilty and deserving of punishment.

This all climaxed one night at a revival service, when the visiting minister told a horrifying story about a movie star who had led a most sinful life. The devil had gotten her soul because of a serious car accident, and her head was found lying on the hood of the car. She was a guilty sinner of course, so her fate was more than justified. This was the straw that broke the camel's back. I ran to the front during the invitation and took

21

the hand of one of the older associate ministers, unable to speak. He asked what I was doing there, but I could not tell him. Pattie managed to get me home, and I was in bed for a week, dying, as far as I was concerned. It was but a short time later that I tried to run my car into the bridge abutment. I didn't care where I went – heaven or hell. I just wanted "out." Such was the state of my life on that eventful day when I tried to end it all. But it was also in that state, in some miraculous way, an "inner voice" allowed me to consider another alternative – a simple thought that there could be a better way. And because I allowed myself to consider there might be another way, I finally sought help.

LOOKING INSIDE

So what had brought me to see Dr. Francis Smith-Jones at her office in the library of a local church in the mid 1980's? Why this healer and not another? This specific therapist had come highly recommended by my best friend and Chief Radiological Technologist, Novelle Weist who was also going through major life changes.

To be honest, I was scared as hell. The realization that I was about to expose myself, in full, to a stranger, a female stranger with whom I would spend several hours each week for the next eight years, was not a comforting thought. According to the therapist's office brochure, it would take six to eight years to make a major personality change. I was to discover that, at least in my case, it was correct. As I was to later understand, there were several reasons my path led me to this particular psychotherapist. It would have made no sense to me at the time, as I had to see it in retrospect.

As a child, I was so dependent on my mother that our local Baptist preacher commented on it. He had told my mother that it was not a good relationship, but neither of us understood what he meant. However, that relationship set the pattern for my need for "women to make me happy," my subconscious way of thinking. Why would seeking a female therapist not also fit into that scheme? Moreover, her office was in a church and she worked with a religious group. Perhaps that would save me from the wrath of God as I exposed my wicked self. God would not kill me and "mother" would not throw me out, no matter how evil I was, or so it seemed to that "unknown" self. Or, maybe the Universe led me there. Who knows? I was there, and it was meant to be. It was just one of those incredible synchronicities which I would eventually come to understand on my journey through life.

The healing process was not going to be cheap. The final cost was about $25,000. Was it worth it? Was I worth it? And all the people said, "Amen!" Some will understand that

statement. Many will not. About half way through my therapy,
I wrote the following poem. The year was 1988.

TO DR. FRANCIS

I know I am no prize to God
Nor hardly one to man,
But surely there is some good in me
Please find it if you can.

I'm reaching out, as I know how
And you extend your hand.
I'm almost there, but "he" interferes,
And I slip through like sand.

Is there some truth I fear to learn,
While struggling with my mind?
A few split seconds I seem to see
The things that you would have me find.

Then "he" steps in, this teenage boy
Who's stronger than the man.
I fear I am no match for him,
Please help me if you can.

You've been so kind, so strong, so firm
And rescued me from briny deep.
There's still much more for me to learn
Before I start eternal sleep.

So, Smith-Jones, don't send away
This boy, this man, this hapless heart.
But by your wit and strength from God
Make one whole man, each one a part.

6

THE RE-CREATION

I suppose there are several titles one could give to this experience. It is the reason for writing this book – to show that no matter who one is, where one is, or what one's environment is, self love can be attained. I am sure there must be many ways to do this, perhaps as many as there are journeys of souls on Earth. And so, even before arriving on this planet, I arranged to do it a particular way. But, that is also another story,

We must return to the first few psychotherapeutic sessions with Francis to really appreciate the changes that were to follow. Those changes were to culminate in my Big Bang on that beautiful day of November 12, 1991, nine years later.

One of the first things my therapist asked me to do was to "go inside." This process of visualization was totally unknown to me. I was told to close my eyes, take fairly deep breaths, and try to visualize the moving air as a white cloud, passing in and out of my nostrils and lungs. After a while I was encouraged to "see" the air going inside of me to my very core, and to then verbalize what I saw.

To my amazement, I found myself in total darkness, as a limbless human embryo, suspended in mid-air, screaming to be touched, to be loved. The experience was terrifying, and quickly brought me back to the reality of the therapy room, and to ample tears. This was repeated many times in the next few months, until it was no longer uncomfortable, but expected. It was not an experience that I wanted to repeat, but seemed to remain unchanged throughout my years of therapy.

Was this the Inner Child of whom I was so afraid? I knew if I unleashed it from its cage, it would destroy me and the world. Or was it a child of beauty?

INNER CHILD

I am here
Can you see me?
Am I a boy or girl?
It does not matter
I am tender, caring, vulnerable
Depending on you for my nourishment

I have always been here
Sometimes hiding, sometimes cowering
But always in need of the love you have
I never learned to play, to trust
I did learn to survive
But not always happy with my choice.

I see you each morning
In the mirror
As you shave and brush your teeth
The bags under your eyes
The frown on your forehead
Are they there because of me?

It is time
Time that we quit suffering
I am very young, but I know
What WE need
Can we hold each other?
Can we be one and stop the pain?

Our Mother-Father Creator
Are waiting for us
With the Power of the Universe
Spinning us around in the mixture of life
Beckoning us with open hearts
To join Them in the stars.

Toward the end of my years of therapy, Francis
suggested it would be good for me to do something, just for
me, without considering the benefit to anyone else, to prove I

loved myself. Having told "self" how much I loved it, many thousands of times, one would think it surely would have caught on by now. The least expensive thing to do, I thought, would be to drive the 200 miles to Dallas, Texas and spend the weekend in the Hotel Weston, at the Galleria. There, I could enjoy the comfort, solitude, and benefits of the mall, just for good old Jim.

I left on a Friday afternoon, and was well situated in my sixteenth floor hotel room by evening, just in time for a marvelous steak in the dining room. After eating, I went to my room to relax and watch some television. When I tried to sleep, I broke out in a sweat, became extremely anxious and began pacing the floor. Fortunately, there were no windows that could be opened, so there was no chance I would fling myself out one and end it all on the pavement below. I still remember, vividly, the unreasonable fear that swept over me. It made no sense at the time.

By 3:00 am, I surrendered to my fears, packed my bag and began the confusing trip home. Arriving early the next morning, about first light, I was greeted at the door by my wife. She asked why I had come back, and the only answer that I could give, not really knowing the why of it, was "I have to mow the lawn." Now, figure that out. It was very simple. In my mind, with my distorted thinking, I did not deserve the weekend in Dallas. I was obligated to be productive, all the time, as any good workaholic knows.

Round 1.

Proving my worth to be loved.
Result – I was KO'ed.

Round 2.

Sex therapy.

I always thought I had a severe problem with sex, and the reason for that will be evident somewhere deep in this book. Suffice it to say, I decided to consult a sex therapist. The only one that seemed to be available was a female psychotherapist at the University of Oklahoma Medical Center.

We met at the center, and then she conducted weekly group sessions at her home which was about half way between Oklahoma City and Tulsa, Oklahoma. More than half the group were psychotherapists from Tulsa, all women. I was totally uncomfortable there, as most of the others seemed to be, but then, that WAS the reason we were there.

The sessions started with the therapist asking each participant to say three good things about themselves, seemingly a relatively easy task. However, most of us could not do it, and would break down in uncontrollable crying during the process. It never got easy. Try as I might, I never could find even one good thing to say about myself. I even wrote a poem about the process, having one of the psychotherapists in mind when I composed it. When I read it out loud during our session, it brought out so much fear in her that she ran from the therapist's home in terror. I had similar experiences with running during these sessions, and fortunately was encouraged to return by other participants sent to my aid.

TELL ME YOUR NAME
AND THREE GOOD THINGS ABOUT YOURSELF

What's good about me? Asked every time
'Tis best to answer in a rhyme
I want to go where sight is true

Past mirrored glass, where all is told
To see what is, be really bold
Like minds gone past
Like Alice Through The Looking Glass

While lurking there, what will I be?
I want to be what I really am
Mad Hatter? Sure. Who gives a damn?

Beyond the pain, beyond despair
With laughter, joy and teddy bear
Will you come, go with me there?

My progress in the group was limited at best, so the therapist suggested that attending a sexual surrogate clinic in

Los Angeles, California would be beneficial. I can't believe I am revealing this, because I never knew there was such a clinic. Just the thought of it made me want to leave the Earth, but I was determined to fix myself no matter what it took. At the clinic, each client was to be furnished with a psychologist, present at all times, and a surrogate sexual partner. The cost was over $5,000, excluding accommodations and travel. I found it hard to believe that I was actually going to go through with it, but I was desperate to make a change in my life.

I made the down payment, purchased an airline ticket, and reserved a hotel room. I was a nervous wreck while making all the arrangements, sort of in a dream world, knowing that God would strike me dead at any moment because of my sinful nature. Just before I was to depart on this strange journey, I was struck with a tremendous fear and cancelled the whole trip.

Shortly thereafter, I received a telephone call from the California psychologist with whom I would have been working. We delved deeply into my situation for over two hours, and he finally told me that I did not have a sexual problem. What a shocking revelation! Apparently, I had severe touch deprivation syndrome, and the psychologist proceeded to explain to me exactly what that meant. It made total sense, as my mind raced to confirm his assessment remembering numerous childhood incidents.

Round 2.

Sex therapy. KO'ed again.

Round 3.

Re-creation.

Round 3 was a bit more fulfilling. My sessions continued with Dr. Smith-Jones, and eventually developed into longer two-hour consultations. I had to have two hours because I would be so devastated and dehydrated from crying I needed time to recuperate in order to return to my office to see patients. As I was leaving Francis's office one afternoon, following the usual two-hour session, a white folder on the corner of her desk caught my eye. It may have been there for days, but for some reason I hadn't noticed it. We will speak of the synchronicities of life later, but noticing that simple folder would play a part in the biggest change of my life I was yet to experience.

For some reason I asked what it was, since there was no writing on it. She said it was some kind of a brochure, and asked me to take it home. I did. I am still amazed that, whatever I may need at a particular time in my life, the necessary assistance and guidance will be furnished to me if I am open to it. This was such a time.

7

THE BIG BANG

The brochure turned out to be a catalog from the Esalen Institute on Big Sur, in Northern California, about 41 miles South of Carmel. Once a place popularized by hippies, it was now a very successful and world recognized institute where one could come and find Self. Or, at least one could search for that elusive part of being within a non-judgmental environment, and actually receive aid in doing this by numerous self-help courses and activities.

There were indoor and outdoor activities, massage, yoga, photography, white water rafting, etc. All had the purpose of finding self-love, the precursor to happiness. As I perused the list of courses, one stood out in particular. It was a course led by a psychotherapist from Los Angeles, whom I call Sly Fox. Each year she offered, and still does, a week's workshop called Change and Self-Esteem. Again, it was very difficult for me to decide to sign up for it and make the necessary traveling arrangements. I did not want a repeat of the failure of Round 1 and Round 2.

For reasons of sanity insurance, Francis had made a cassette tape, which she asked me to play when the time was correct. She told me that I would know when that time was. "Sure," I thought, "I could do that." She also told me that nothing HAD to happen, that just planning to go, and going there, was a victory in itself.

I tried to get Pattie to go with me, but in her wisdom she insisted that it must be done just for me and not for the sake of someone else. It reminded me of the time when I had asked my brother-in-law (whom I consider a brother and also a very productive workaholic), what he did just for himself. His answer, which proved my point, was, "I help others."

I think I was in a daze, or perhaps a coma, as I boarded the jet, and flew toward the Pacific Ocean to eventually land at Monterey, California. Something was different. I felt strange, as if I weighed only half of what I did in Oklahoma. Each time I land in at Monterey, I experience that same feeling.

It was fun checking out a rental car to make the trip to Esalen, via Carmel. Being a talker, I made friends with the rental clerk, and we continued our friendship over the six trips I made to Esalen. I always wore the same jeans jacket that had been painted on the back by my wife's cousin, Becky. She is an inspired artist, and the illustration she had drawn was that of a serpent (signifying the Year of the Snake) with a Native American headdress. It was truly striking, and could not go unnoticed. In the following years on return visits, as I wandered through the same airports, the clerks would say, "Hey! I recognize that jacket." It was another way to make energy contact with others, a process of which I was unaware for many years.

The trip down Highway 1 was an awesome experience. I felt the energy of the mighty ocean waves, the depth of the blueness of the water of Monterey Bay, and the land itself suddenly rising above sea level to become mountains covered by the spirituality of the giant Redwood trees. The city roads gave way to the curvaceous and narrow mountain roads lapping over the cliffs that plunged into the sea. I could see why so many had run off the road to perish in the rocks and water below. It took a great deal of effort to stay in the car and remain focused in my body, but I managed to do so.

Now, you would think I would have been ready to reach the Esalen Institute, nestled between highway and ocean, but obscured by vegetation. I was a bit surprised by the fear that arose within as I saw the gateway to my salvation. I just could not go in. I drove for hours, up and down the costal highway, trying to muster the courage to enter the forbidden area where people ran free and sometimes naked. Surely God would destroy me if I went to such a place. However, practicality and greed finally won out as I started down the steep incline to the check-in shack. I thought to myself, "Did this person, who gave me directions to the main office, see me as I saw myself – a sinful, quivering being who knew all of his past would soon be exposed to the Universe?" Nah! He was barely awake enough to check me in. So much for my assumed importance, it was supposed to be "all about me."

I silently checked in at the main office, receiving my room key, trying to appear invisible. It took some time to realize that most, if not all, of the visitors at Esalen were working on their own individual journeys. Even the staff members were on personal quests of self-discovery.

In the dark recesses of my mind was a hope that a mistake had been made in scheduling room mates, and my room mate would be woman. Good thing that did not happen or I would have been racing back through the front gate, in abject fear. Remember the touch deprivation syndrome? This was part of it, the fear of being touched, especially by a woman even though I definitely yearned for it.

I was the first to check into the small three-bed room, which really had space for only two beds. I was a bit concerned about what my roommates would think of me, forgetting that they were there with their own problems, and not concerned with mine. This became very evident as the first roommate appeared.

In his late twenties, he had a full head of dark brown hair and a full beard, both of which I disliked because of my obvious baldness. I tried to conceal my lack of hair with a fine hairpiece, which the supplying company insisted on calling a hair system. It was held tightly in place, bound to the thin rim of remaining hair that extended, like the edge of a bowl, around the sides and back of my head. Actually, it was so natural in appearance, that the lady who later massaged me did not know it was false until she stumbled over one of the knots. That would probably be considered a fine hairpiece.

Okay, I will go ahead and say something about this wig. It was yet another part of my life masquerade, trying to hide what I perceived as my true and most pitiful identity. I had never really wanted it, although I did crave having a fine head of hair as most men do. Several years before, as my wife and our two young sons were walking through a local shopping mall, one of the kids yelled, "Dad! There's your hair!" I turned

33

to see a gentleman, standing in the common area just outside the hair place, combing a graying wig. The three of them overpowered me, and soon I had a fine crop of new hair, nestling on a once bald spot. Again, I was doing something for someone else, which in itself is not so bad, but in my case was just another indicator of me not being myself.

I did finally graduate to a more professional hairpiece that was securely fastened to my head by cord or glue, and maintained by a beautiful young lady named Miss Vicki. Maintaining an expensive hairpiece turned out to be an appropriate way for me to receive some human touching without any obligations. And, I was able to help Vicki with her own personal image problems from time to time. All in all, the whole process was just so much justification on my part for genuine human interaction.

Now, where did that first roommate go? Oh, there he is, sitting opposite me on the edge of his bed, about two feet away. For some reason, he started laying out his life for me, a total stranger, as if I were a priest and he were confessing. I have been told that I have that effect on people. He confessed that he was a pedophile, and had been unsuccessfully treated for it. He had been in a local monastery for several years, and was now serving as priest in a boy's school. "Not the best place for him to be," I thought. He was also gay, and I had no problem with that, unless he picked me as a lover. I couldn't even love myself, so certainly could not be open to someone caring for me. As luck would have it, he was my first massage partner in our class work. The massage was uneventful as I tried to put away thoughts of where he was, and where I was, and what if, and on and on.

He left the room while I remained sitting, reeling from information overload about a subject totally foreign to me. I was only too happy to keep it that way. All this was taking place in a cozy little cabin, perched on a hill overlooking the ocean. The crashing of the waves against the rocks seemed to be magnified within the room. In spite of my feelings of discomfort, I refused any thought of changing campus rooms. As soon as he left, another young man entered the cabin, slightly larger and taller than the first. His energy felt more obvious than the first, and was somewhat disturbing. I was to be father confessor, again. Another story concerning sex, but at least his issue was an overwhelming desire to have relations with the opposite sex, and with an adult. There is a word for this dysfunction that I cannot remember, but it is an abnormal desire for sex that never leaves and is never satisfied. Looking for something that is not there? Trying to find the right woman to make one happy? Whatever one calls it, it is ultimately a search for inner peace. But looking for it outside of one's self always ends in failure.

I was able to be of assistance when my second roommate awakened me one night with violent snoring. I immediately knew that he had a serious medical problem, an obstruction of the upper airway due to loose tissue in that area. Known as sleep apnea, it causes sleep deprivation, and can be suddenly fatal. Doctor to the rescue! I jumped out of bed, awakened the half-sleeping patient and explained to him what was going on. On returning home, he actually had the curative surgery and, I hope, lived happily ever after.

Did I tell you that it was Sunday in this story? Well, it was, and that even increased my anxiety as I was caught up in the "do's" and "don'ts" of organized religion. So, here I was, in a sinful place, listening to sinful people on a Holy Day. And, I hadn't even gone to church!

I had arrived at Esalen a bit too early to check in at the office. After meeting my two roommates, I decided to walk around the grounds and try to go to the ocean's edge. That would take some doing since most of the grounds are very high above the ocean. By just following my intuition, which I didn't know I had at the time, I ventured down a narrow asphalt path, over a small creek and proceeded toward the Big House, one of the lodges.

From the other direction came this short and pretty red headed lady, about forty years of age. We met at the crosswalk and it seemed a natural thing to say, "Hi, how are you? What are you doing here?" She told me that her name was Gale and she was from Canada, a doctor's wife, and that her marriage was not going well. Her trip here was to "find herself." I sort of knew what that meant. She also asked, "Do you know the way to the ocean?" I didn't, but we decided to proceed together, hand in hand, and soon found ourselves on a redwood deck next to a very long and steep, steel stairway at the edge of the ocean. We decided to stay where we where and swap life stories.

I can't remember how, but I seemed to be able to help her find some answers even when I could not find my own. I think that might be the plight of many psychotherapists. We then proceeded along the path back towards the common area where the office, pool and dining room were located. Before we got there, we passed by the pool, very close to the edge of the cliff and stopped at a grassy spot as she told me about her best childhood friend, a Japanese girl with whom she became very close. The girl had taught her a song in that language and Gale still remembered it. The friend had moved to Japan not long after that. For some reason, I made Gale close her eyes, look with her Mind's Eye over the ocean to Japan and sing the song, out loud. It was so touching, her contact with her friend in this way, that we both cried. That was not in the tour guide.

She decided she wanted to return the favor and help me with my problem. I was afraid of nudity and I even avoided looking at a naked body. That may seem strange since I was a practicing physician and frequently saw naked people. But, that was different because I always went into the "doctor mode" and became aloof to sexuality, Always.

We continued down the path as Gale held my hand to give me courage, behind the dining room, going slightly downhill to the baths. The massage area was also there, and there was no attempt to cover naked bodies while being massaged or while in the very hot water of the rock and concrete tubs. We came to the entrance, still holding hands, and I did not die. Chalk one up for my side. Thank you very much.

I only saw Gale one more time while revisiting Esalen. She made a special trip from a visit to California to see me, since she knew that I would be there. I was wearing a large and heavy monk's type robe when I happened onto her on the path

36

by the creek. We said nothing, just embraced and all that needed to be conveyed was done by non-verbal communication, as she thanked me for being there for her and as I made the same statement. I wonder how she is doing these days. I wonder if she is again riding the black stallion across the sands in front of the Egyptian pyramids, as she does each time she visits that exotic country.

The same evening that I arrived at Esalen, met Gale the first time and observed nudity, we had our first meeting with Sly Fox, leader of the group. I was already exhausted by all that I had experienced, and the damn workshop hadn't even begun. Encountering a pedophile and sex-obsessed addict, while wedged into an undersized oceanfront cabin, had already pushed me to the limit. What else could there be to end this perfect day? I found out, and the beginning of the Big Bang started.

Sly Fox outlined the week's activities. We were scheduled for two-hour meetings, three times a day, PRN. I had to throw the "PRN" thing in to prove I am a doctor. That means "as needed." I was okay with it until she got to Tuesday evening. On Tuesday, she informed the group that we would go to the baths and do nude body painting. I was incredulous, and raised my hand like a proper little child and said, "You may do that. I will not."

There were twenty one participants in the group, the women outnumbering the men, and had come from different parts of the United States and from around the world. A few were from the movie industry in LA. Looking back on it, we would have made a good crew for a pirate ship.

Sly Fox asked us to "go inside," and I was so delighted that I understood how to do something "appropriate" in what I considered such a strange place. I could do that, as I had done this exercise for several years with Dr. Smith-Jones. Of course, I knew I could go inside and would see my old, miserable friend, the limbless embryo. There was some strange comfort in that. But in spite of my certainty, I was about to be surprised.

Instead of the embryo without arms or legs, suspended in blackness, I was in a well-lighted room, much like a corporate boardroom. In the middle was a large oak table with chairs. In each chair was a part of my personality, which made fifteen chairs in total. Many aspects of "Jim" were there, including the embryo in mother's womb listening in fear as I heard my parents yelling during one of their frequent fights.

Perhaps that is why I resisted being born, and a serious uterine tear resulted. I recall, early in life, asking my mother if she loved me. She quickly answered, "Of course I love you. I almost died when you were born." Great! I almost killed my mother; was my interpretation of those events. What a joy it was going to be to carry that knowledge the rest of my life. I was constantly reminded of that fact each time mother had uterus problems, which was often, until she had a hysterectomy years later.

MISSING PARTS
July 15. 1988

She died to me when I was born
And expelled from uterus torn
Just in the way and not desired
Better had this one not been sired

There is a void that was never filed
A work of love that was never killed
But since it was not ever offered
It follows that it was not proffered

To build on something that was not there
A trait that should be nursed with care
This trait was never given a chance
Instead of love was given a lance

Learn to love and to be loved
A thought into my mind is shoved
There is no basis to begin
There is no start, there is no end

38

What do I do to feel this joy?
That I never felt as a little boy
Simply in love to hold one near
My empty heart would greatly cheer

I'm struggling now to build a tower
For which I do not have the power
'Tis hard to build a tinker toy part
Without the toys nor where to start

While my embryo "part" occupied one chair, there were still fourteen other parts present in my guided "inner journey." The oldest being the fifteen-year-old who had figured out how bad life was going to be, and decided he would stick with that. He was the one who decided at that age that life would be suffering, and hoped he did not wake up at age sixty and find out he had done it all wrong. He didn't. He woke up at sixty-two.

All was chaos, as each aspect of me was pounding the table, wanting to be heard. There was no chairman of the board; nothing was organized. Well, I thought, at least this corporate boardroom was better than the kid without arms or legs. At least I could see what was going on. Each time we went inside for the next couple of days, the scene remained the same, and I wondered how long this one would last.

Monday's sessions were unique. The leader used different methods to get to know who we were as we unknowingly exposed ourselves to the group. Each of us had to take a turn sitting in the center and explain to the group why we were there. That was boring to me, since I knew why I was there, and I didn't really care to hear the comments of the others.

When the time came for my pedophile roommate to let it all hang out, so to speak, he immediately began asking for help. He was about as well received as a child molester in a prison setting. However, the attack was verbal instead of physical. I thought the behavior of the group was inappropriate at the time, but I did not speak up. I was so wrapped up in my

39

issues, and my stress, I was barely managing to keep my own head above water.

The first method the leader had for us to start finding ourselves was to have us draw a picture of our immediate family. We were to include the entire family and depict our house in the background as our memories served. While painting is not my forte, I could make a fairly good stick-man, and proceeded to do what I was told to do. Then, each of us was supposed to stand up in turn and show our picture and talk about our family history. When my turn came, all went well until I finished and several group members asked me where my brother was. Good grief! I had totally left him out of the picture. Could that be important? Oh yeah!

Tuesday morning came, and what a beautiful morning it was. Our leader decided that we would meet and meditate on the slightly damp, lush green grass overlooking the eighty foot cliff that rushed to join the ocean. We were in a shaded area next to the impressive Monterey pines.

We formed a circle, lying on our backs, heads pointed inward, with shoulders almost touching. Sly Fox gently tapped a bell and the soothing sound beckoned us to once again go inside. But, I didn't. Instead, I noticed, with some part of me, an undulating soft and bluish-white, ghostly image arising over my body. My immediate response, since I thought I was nuts anyway, was to say "Hey! We are supposed to go inside." To my utter astonishment, a voice answered back, "Don't worry. We will be back, with Love." Okay, now I knew I had flipped, but decided to just let it happen. The worst I could do would be to run rampant like a maniac and jump off the cliff. Nothing like this had ever happened to me before. And being a rigid Baptist fundamentalist and workaholic physician, "going with the flow" was something I was not accustomed to doing. But, somewhere, a decision was made to let it play out.

I was aware of my physical position on the ground, but also aware of another part of my greater self doing something strange. "Nothing to lose" became the functional phrase of the day. As you read this account, I know you will have your own interpretation as to what the following scenes signified.

The misty essence turned into a beautiful male sea gull that flew quickly away and soared for a bit over the ocean with the other sea gulls. It landed on a small outcropping midway up the cliff which was covered with green grass. As it stood there, a large and juicy worm crawled by and was allowed to pass, unafraid.

Flying again, the gull landed on a large limb of one of the Monterey pines. Soon, a female sea gull landed beside him. They quickly built a nest and, as time had no authority in this realm, a pristine white egg appeared. As they watched the egg, it began to vibrate. A crack formed and grew wider and wider until the egg burst asunder.

I suddenly found myself inside the egg looking out as I saw my parents for the first time, beautiful and loving, as was I. I cannot adequately say in words the awesome love energy that overtook me at this time. Perhaps you can remember some time in your own existence where the feeling of love was overpowering. I grew quickly, and it was not long before they were teaching me to fly and to play in the sky with other gulls. I was having trouble with soaring however, and they placed me between them as they gracefully and effortlessly showed me how to soar. I was flapping my wings in disharmony and felt very clumsy as they told me to just relax and go with the flow. It became easy as I followed their guidance.

I quickly learned to dive, and that was exciting. Once, while doing a dive, I heard a beautiful sound. It took me some time to realize that it was my own voice, and that I was singing! But the voice of my father soon replaced mine. "It is time to go back to Jim," he said. The three gulls approached the meditating group, and then hovered above my physical form. Turning back into the shimmering blue-white apparition, they went "inside."

I returned to the familiar room still brightly lit. Something, however, had changed. The boardroom table and chairs containing my various personalities were gone, as well as the former chaos. Now, there was only one large oak chair remaining. On it sat a beautiful young man, wearing a white robe, and smiling. Ah, the Chairman of the Board.

41

At that moment, the bell to return rang, and I jumped up and started yelling, "You won't believe what just happened to me! I must be going crazy! I must write this down before I forget it! (As if I ever would.) I don't have any paper!" Someone quickly tore a page from their notebook and handed it to me, with a pen. I stood there, just looking at the paper and realized that there was no way that I could calm down long enough to write anything.

"I've got to go!" was my next brilliant statement, and I ran off to the garden and woods to talk to the birds, bees, plants and all of nature. I knew that they would understand what I had just experienced. I was sure the group thought, "Aha! Another lunatic." But, I was to find out later that they were excited with me, and sought their own similar re-birth.

Over the years, my seeking to discover the meaning of my experience led me to several conclusions. It does not matter if those conclusions were right or wrong, since the spiritual breakthrough that occurred that Tuesday morning was, and still is, beyond words.

Perhaps though, one meaning of the gull allowing the worm to pass unscathed could be found in the Christian Bible when it talks of the lamb lying down with the lion. Or, another meaning could be to show how one should honor the journey of another. Fun to think about, but there is no need to dwell on it unless the reader has a better idea and can apply it to their personal life.

Later that morning, I took a nap, which now seems ludicrous following an experience of such magnitude. As I lay down, I remembered the "emergency cassette tape" that Francis had sent. This was the time for listening. It was very calming as she told me that nothing had to happen at Esalen, but just to be open to whatever came. Great strides in my therapy had been made, just because I had decided to come to this place.

But, great things DID happen. I was highly energized as I lay there. I began experimenting with feeling my energy between outstretched hands as someone had told me one could do. It was an awesome feeling as the "golden ball" of energy almost forced my hands apart as I expanded and contracted it, threw it in the air and caught it. Oh. Oh. Oh. Crazy again.

I was too full of the energy of the Universe to eat lunch. However, I did go to the swimming pool. Even though it was out in the open near the office and dining room, I proceeded to disrobe totally and swim. I had never done this before, and was unconcerned that I was in plain sight of many people. Not what you would expect from a Baptist Deacon.

It was a very freeing experience. I lay on the wooden deck by the pool, closed my eyes and felt as if I had been born again at the age of four. That was the age that I had been sexually abused by teenage girls. I had been told this by someone also involved at the time and several years older and while I could not remember it, my personality was certainly suggestive of such a happening. Perhaps I had gotten back what had been taken from me.

As I lay there, eyes closed, I became aware of soul stirring music. It was drumming, and was coming from the other side of the pool. I opened my eyes long enough to see that an African drum group had set up and was playing rhythms totally unfamiliar to me.

This was my first introduction to the drum, and it will forever be a part of me. I got up and started dancing, again with my eyes closed, and soon I heard applause. I had to see from whence it came, and was a bit surprised to see two beautiful young women from Brazil dancing with me, also nude. It was not a sexual experience, but it was as if we were small children, playing a game and laughing. This did not seem like the guy that a few days earlier had refused to consider doing body painting at the baths. Later in the afternoon, while having a coffee break in the dining room, I found our leader sitting there. She slyly said, "Rumor has it that you were seen at the pool this morning." That type of remark was why I named her Sly Fox.

Tuesday rolled around and the body painting exercises as well. "Will he do it?" cried the announcer! Yes, he did it. It was so natural, so fun and so non-sexual, for me. I do not know

43

what it meant to the others. I just felt that if it had turned into a sexual experience, as it might have with the Brazilian girls, then I could have regressed to the time when my innocence had been invaded at age four. I thank the Universe that did not happen. Instead, I experienced the freedom of natural joy in spontaneous action. I actually painted the ample breasts of a woman and later washed them off, all of us laughing constantly. I forgot what part of me was painted, and if I could remember, it would be none of your business (grin).

It's amazing to think I had only been at Esalen two days and my world had already completely changed. I had no idea just how much. It is worth noting that it is almost, if not completely, impossible to know where one is in life without a mirror, some one or some thing to reflect the changes we go through. I could not have had my old and new self side by side and made an intelligent comparison, even if that were possible. That seems to remain true to this day. I enjoy others telling me that I have changed, some saying I have totally lost my mind. It is a joy to be able to turn to the latter and say, "That is your problem, not mine."

At Esalen, nobody was crazy, except all those outside the confines of the camp. The support and encouragement was most welcome, but a few might have been jealous of me since I got what they came for.

Sly Fox offered the course *Change and Self Esteem* at Esalen each summer, and I have recommended it to many. In fact, I must tell you at this time of an incident when I did suggest that someone attend her workshop. Following four trips to the Esalen Institute, I was returning home in one of the very large jumbo jets. I requested a seat next to the aisle since I have a bone disease in one leg and use a cane. I got one with only one other seat next to it adjacent to the outer wall. The seat to my left was vacant, and I wondered what exciting experience would happen this time, as happens on all my trips as I meet new souls.

A very pretty young lady approached, in her thirties, and indicated the empty seat was hers. As she passed in front of me, I felt her strong energy field and knew it would be okay to say, "You sure do have a powerful energy field!" She did not take it as a flirtation line. I was relieved at that.

"I have been told that before. I just don't know what to do with it," she replied. From somewhere deep inside me the impulse to speak arose, and my voice said, "Sit down, and I will tell you what to do." Hey! I normally don't tell people what to do, but in this instance, the Universe evidently wanted me to do just that.

I suggested she first read the book *Celestine Prophecy* by James Redfield, and then get an Esalen catalog and take a week workshop called *Change and Self Esteem* by my former teacher. We talked about energy, "people energy," for the rest of the flight and it was a wonderful mutual sharing. Both of us were overcharged by the time we reached our destination. I thought no more of our conversation until I received a ten page letter from her three months later.

She did what I suggested, read the book and took the workshop. It changed her life. She became a writer and a person who believed in herself. She did it, not me. Perhaps I was the catalyst to start the chemical reaction. It does not matter.

I remember one group of five women in our workshop who where most impressed with the radical experience through which I went and one young lady even said my experiences could be made into a movie. Of course, she was from the entertainment industry and had been the trip planner for several musical stars including Mick Jaeger. How could I not puff up a little with that kind of support?

A young producer, also a participant in the workshop, was quite intimidating with his constant reference to his practice of Aikido. His bravado was enhanced by the many bruises he displayed to prove he had been doing it for some time. I have since learned that this kind of bruising is not normal.

This guy was so intimidating that he once, while trying to tell me something, placed his very strong hand on my shoulder, letting me know there was little muscle between his hand and my bones. I don't want to tell you this, but to be quite honest, I talk too much. Always have. Always will. That did not suit him well as he stated, "Don't speak until I tell you to!" Hey! This little old man knows when to be quiet.

He proceeded to unload his negative energy upon me, the first time I was aware that one could actually feel energy coming from a human being. I was ready to go back and talk to the girls. Do you know what? I was so interested in him from a medical standpoint that I had the audacity to tell him the next day that he should see his doctor because he may be suffering from spontaneous bruising, a subconscious self infliction of trauma to one's body in a severe state of agitation. That is, if there is any truth to that idea. Thank God, he didn't hit me but took it seriously.

"How negative was he?" you ask. This man radiated such strong negativity that it was noticed by most of the group. He was so negative that his "downbeat vibes" were experienced from a considerable distance the next day as we hiked along the Tanbark Trail, home to the beautiful redwood trees and is magnificent beyond words. So if you had been there, you would have definitely remembered it as a unique and wonderful experience.

Sly Fox had taken us to her church, a shady pool surrounded by the ancient, redwood trees. On the way, we walked about thirty feet apart trying to remain in a meditative mood. The lady behind me quickened her pace, caught up to me and said, "I don't want to look, but I think Jack (for want of a better name) is behind me. I feel a great negative force following me." Sure enough, there he was. I would love to know what happened to him; I think.

When we got to the "church" Sly Fox told us to pick out one of the trees, then to go to our tree and to meditate. Of course, being the gentleman that I always tried to be, saving the best and easiest for the girls, I dragged the old body to the tree that was the most difficult to reach. It was a grand old thing, and I saw it sort of like a grandfather. I nestled easily in its coarse folds of bark, with room to spare, and started the meditation. After a time, soft laughter reached my ears, and in my mind's eye, I looked to see from whence it came.

The laughter seemed to be coming from behind several of the trees, and it was not long until I saw dark skinned young Braves peering out from behind them. Here we go again, I thought, Nutsville. It did not take long for them to gather around me and do a "welcome to the tribe" dance. I was given the name Littlegull and considered myself a member of the Esselen Indian tribe henceforth. The Redwoods became my "spirit trees" and I intend to spend some time in one of them when I pass, if any are left. In fact, I was so impressed with them that I wrote the following poem.

FLY WILD

Fly wild, fly wild
My sweet sea gulls
To the Esselen Indian spirits
In the trees
In the trees of red
Of two thousand years.
My tribe, my tribe
How I long to be with you
With your simple truths
Your simple pleasures.
Fly wild, fly wild
Circle the trees that hold my brothers
The spirits that give
Me strength to live
And hope that I too
Might find the oneness
With Mother Earth and Father Sun
How I long to be with you
Mother, father and tiny bird
That my re-birth did make
On those slopes of old
Near boiling bath
My brother surf still calls my name
As tiny whale plays silly game
Littlegull, Littlegull
I am you, I AM you

Since this is a book about energy, spirit energy, soul energy, body energy, etc. about which I know little, but with which I have had many wonderful experiences, I would like to tell of some incidents concerning a female shaman's class.

I have always had strong feelings that I was a Native American in some past life. During my third or fourth trip to Esalen, I took a course given by a female shaman from South America. It included a method of healing using spirit energies, and we practiced on each other. During a lull, a young lady from Mexico asked the leader if she did channeling. The answer was that she could, but she had never been asked to do it before.

The Mexican girl wanted to contact her deceased father. Apparently, when she was a little girl, her father had been murdered in the room adjacent to hers. Maria told us to go to our safe place, and while I was quite ignorant in metaphysical talk, I understood what she meant. This was to keep errant spirits from trying to enter a body open to anything that might be flying by. The channeling was a success and the young lady was most grateful.

About ten minutes later, however, a young Esalen worker said that he felt very ill and was about to throw up. He did and then began having seizures. The leader said he had been too open, which he later admitted since he wanted something to happen. In other words, he was possessed, according to her, and I was not going to argue with that. It took her and two other shamans about three hours to rid him of the unwanted intruder. I don't know if there is any truth to this, but it was extremely impressive.

One of the class participants was a physician from Los Angeles, a pathologist and also a coroner for the city. He had developed metastatic cancer of the skin and had come in order to try to be healed or heal himself. He was not a joyful little man, and with my life history I could understand that. Evidently, he was not ready to "cast off his mortal coil."

He asked Maria to try a healing session on him. It was a most impressive scene as it was twilight, and the remaining members of the group were standing on a redwood deck overlooking the Pacific Ocean. We were looking through a sliding glass door as Maria worked on the doctor, the only ones in the room. There was one naked light bulb suspended from the ceiling in the center of the room. Not a peep was heard as we observed the session, hoping and praying for a miracle. None of us had yet come to that place where we realized that healing is our natural state of being.

As human beings, most of us have simply blocked our natural ability to release healing energies. The truth is that each of us has all the necessary "inner" resources to manifest complete healing regardless of the particular illness. Wow, what a time to throw that in! Don't leave me now, there is much more to come.

Suddenly, someone in the group whisper-yelled "Look! On the floor, beneath the light bulb!" There was a most lovely giant moth, as if it had come off the picture on the cover of a Carlos Castaneda's book. I had never seen such a moth, yet many of us were aware of the significance of its appearance. There is a saying that goes, "Where the giant moth is, there can be no negativity." I am sure this is paraphrased, but it makes the point. Even this skeptic old bugger was impressed. No, I do not know the results of the session or if the physician is still living. I do know that this brought me closer to the reality of spirit.

In this particular class, we were required to pick a partner. That always seemed to be the way at these things, and it was the part with which I was usually uncomfortable. It was sort of like being the skinny little kid in grade school, and no one picking you for their team. Well, this was no different. I was old, bald and totally unaware of what was going on around me during the workshops. I usually tried to pick someone whom no one else might want, someone like me (that old poor self esteem thing again).

Before I could find that person, I was picked by a very pretty young lady whose mother was the director of the Massage school at Esalen. "This cannot be," I told this old self, but was delighted when it did happen. Of course, I had to reason it out that she felt sorry for me. Man, did I have a lot to learn, and still do.

I was on the table first, and one of the first motions that we did was to have the standing partner place their hands over the Third Eye of the reclining partner. There was no touching, and the energy was to be felt through the space between the hand and forehead.

My eyes were closed, and I saw this faint blue light in my mind's eye. It also felt as if my partner's fingers were going into my forehead and deep into my brain. There was no pain, just a pleasant sensation. I was not going to say anything about what I felt, wishing to appear sane. But as we were debriefing later, she made this most interesting statement. "Jim, when I was standing over you with my hands over your Third Eye, I felt that my hands were going into your head and there was this blue light." Well, knock me over with a feather! If that is not confirmation of something, I might as well stop writing right now.

We all deal with limitations in our physical forms, and as for me, I have Paget's disease of the left tibia (big lower leg bone) with resultant non-healing fractures, pain and a host of other associated issues as part of the package.

Knowing about my condition, Maria decided she wanted to work on my leg. The group gathered around as I closed my eyes and she began her thing. I was astounded by the force of her non-touching hands, as I almost had to hold onto the table to keep from being pushed off (wish I could do that – and at will). When I felt her at my feet, the pushing pressure was awesome. It felt as if the left side of my body was drawing up, and then I heard Maria let out an affirming "AH!" I did not open my eyes. Later, as I talked to the group, trying to find out what they observed, no one could tell me except to say that my left side just seemed to go "Whoosh!" So, I am left with that and noticed no definite change in the leg. I did write a poem about my leg, and if you will allow me, will insert it here.

ODE TO MY LEFT LEG

You've served me well these three score years
Through many joys and many tears
Taken for granted most of the time
You have, for the most part, stayed in your prime.

Perhaps at eight, when spears in dreams
Lanced through your length in painful streams
With foot turned in, you tried to warn
Less than perfect this leg was born.

51

While running jumping, climbing trees
You did quite well with helping knees
Till on that day on Bunny Hill
We lost our cool on a forward spill.

The "straw that broke the camel's back"
A twist, a turn and a spiral crack
You bowed your shaft and struggled on
For twenty three years from dawn to dawn.

You did your best and gave your most
But now you must give up the ghost
I'm proud of you, and the rest of me
Will care for you till we cross that sea

We'll pass it on to the next of kin
This bone disease called "Saber Shin."

Oh! Oh! I almost forgot to tell you about where I went when Maria asked us to go to our "safe place." I had not done that before, but immediately, in my mind's eye (I like that phrase), I was suddenly a little Native American boy in the very area where Esalen resides. I was playing with a little white and black spotted dog, and my mother was sitting on the grass not far away, working with a basket, smiling at my antics. Father was standing a bit further off, with arms crossed and legs spread, also watching the play. See, I told you I was an Esselen Indian in a past life. What other proof would you need? It would be less confusing if I told you that the Institute where I had my awesome experiences is spelled "Esalen" while the Indian Tribe is spelled "Esselen."

This idea about being an Esselen Indian in a past life was evidently very important to me. I was recently reading in the Monterey Herald about how most individuals believed the tribe was extinct. But not long ago, several tribal members had re-surfaced because of a threat to their ancient tribal land. Someone had proposed that a dam be built on a river that ran through the land near a large boulder called the "Birthing Rock." It was at this rock that the young women would come when ready to go into labor and deliver their child. I had a distinct impression that I had been delivered there in that long ago life, the number sticking in my mind being about 2000 years ago.

I was uncomfortably outraged about this proposed incursion on "our" land. In a dream, a poem came to me about the birthing rock, its endangerment and a plea to stop the building of the dam. The poem was published in the Monterey Herald, much to my amazement. Jan Penny, my good friend from Carmel, California had put me in touch with the poetry editor of the newspaper, and her assistance made the publication of the following poem possible.

THE CALL

August 23, 1993

The drums, the drums
Vibration hums the ancient call to fight
To save that spot where my bones lie
The sacred grave where all my tribe
In secret rest beneath the sky
Of night and day

Who sounds the call?
Who makes the threat?
That shakes the holy ground
Away, away from here you who do not
Understand
And tear from us this sacred land

The guardian giants
Have long been near
Their red shafts guard like loving spear
But even they in all their might
Are vanquished, slain by steel
No where to rest but in man made form

Would you take my home?
With all that I have loved
The loving child, the tender mate
The Spirit trees
That holds my Braves
And graves that hold our bones

What kind of man
That cannot see
That progress made of hate and cold
Destroys our humanity
That tears this down to build that up
The spirit lost in this

You've stirred our souls
We rise again
This Esselen tribe that you have waked
Not only now but lives of past
Make known their ire in what you do
Withdraw and give us peace

8

DISCOVERING THE DRUM

There will be a lot in this book about African drumming. It has been my tool for slipping up on people in order to help them lose their fear of death and to help them drop their judgments. Drumming also assists them to be open to all that the Universe has for them – not exactly a small task. Another way to express it is to help others find out who they are and love what they find. I like that.

During my first Esalen trip, I glanced at the bulletin board where a note telling of African drum lessons was displayed. As I was to discover, this was going to be yet another important synchronicity in my life. The note explained that one hour of the class was $40, which seemed a bit steep to spend on self. The lesson was to be given by Heather, a young Esalen staff member, at the Barn near the beach, the only area that was at beach level. Even though I was debating with myself over the cost of the class versus my own value, I finally decided to attend.

The class met at the far end of the camp, and a pleasant stroll eventually brought me there. Heather was conducting her class in an old barn which had been converted to living quarters. As I approached, hearing drumming, I sat down on a bench by a fire pit and waited for my turn. The drumming stopped and a long shadow passed over me as I looked up to see the source. It was Heather. She was exceptionally tall and thin, and wore wrinkled shorts and shirt. I did not see her as a pretty person at all, but used my typical human judgment and put her in the "don't date" category. It goes without saying that my biased and limited perceptions were still active and running strong at the time.

Inside Heather had three fairly large djembes (African drums) and said she would teach me two basic strokes, but not the slap or pa ta as one of my teachers calls the sound. First, we both drummed like children, without rhythm, modulation or respect for the hands. That was fun, and warmed me up. For just a wee moment, I was a kid again. She taught me the bass and tone, two separate sounds that were fairly easy to do. The hour went very fast, and as I looked up from the drum as we finished, I saw a very beautiful woman sitting beside me. What had happened? Had she changed? Of course not, I had changed. Was it from the drum, her energy or what? I cannot say, but it was a most welcome discovery. My love for the drum has never abated from that moment.

I don't know what happened to my roommates after my first Esalen visit. I suppose they lived through all that went on. Oh yes, I do know that the big fellow had a few sexual trysts. I was ready to dash home to Oklahoma and tell all that had happened. Many changes confirmed that something had really happened. I no longer had migraine headaches, had lost my fear of heights, no more mal de mer and certainly was no longer afraid of nudity. Even food tasted better as I started learning to take in the wonders of Earth. My last breakfast consisted of some kind of small melon and other fresh fruits. The lady sitting on the other side of the table said "You sure do look like you are enjoying that melon." It was surprising that she would say that, and it awakened me to the truth of the statement. Melon had never tasted better. The melon and I became one.

The trip back to Monterey was even better than the one to Esalen, the colors of Nature more vivid, the ocean more energetic. It was even more difficult to stay in the car. The flight to the LA Airport was pleasant and uneventful. I think that I was in the airplane most of the time. You remember the three sea gulls that were part of my re-birth? Well, they were flying with me and wanted to be outside the airplane, so I let them soar free if they agreed to come back to me. Now, don't roll your eyes back like that. I will be okay.

The trip from LA to Oklahoma City was one of the roughest I have ever experienced, but it "seemed" to me to be the calmest flight I had ever taken. The food was excellent, and I didn't even have to wear an earphone to know exactly what was going on in the overhead movie. I knew just what the characters were saying and feeling. When I told the hostess how good the food was, she looked at me rather strangely. As we disembarked, I got a second strange look as I told the Captain that it was the best ride I had ever had. Little did they know what was going on inside me. Little did I know myself.

Pattie picked me up at the Oklahoma City airport about 12:30 AM, after my three gulls had returned. I tried to be silent and not share what had happened, since I was not sure what HAD happened and how Pattie would receive it. Silly me, there was way too much stirring inside to not let it out. I would have exploded. When we got to the house, we sat on the floor in front of the fireplace (we never do that and especially when there is no fire) and I began to try to tell her some of my experience. When I finished, she started sharing things about herself (she never did that) and I asked why she did at this time. Her answer was, "Because you have learned to listen." Just blew me away. Of course, I am not sure I listen that much and I have many witnesses to confirm my ability to talk a lot. She did say that I was not the same person that she had married. Taking a great chance I asked, "Do you like the old guy or the new guy?" I could finally breathe when she replied, "The new guy." Do I hear sweet music playing?

9

LEARNING TO LOVE

You must know that my re-creation experience had to have influenced my marriage. Well, of course, it did in a most dramatic and wonderful way. And here is where I answer the question you have probably thought of asking more than once, "If you didn't like Pattie while in school, then why in the world did you marry her?" Thank you for that question. And I will get to the answer, but for now it allows me to continue that part of the story and tell you about some of my beliefs. Don't you just hate it when an author does that?

I want to make it clear that I DO have beliefs, but I do not have a belief system. It might be better to call them "knowings." There is a great difference, in my opinion. In fact, I no longer have a compulsion to be correct since I am not trying to impress anyone. I gained self-approval, self-love in my Esalen experience, and therefore do not have to have the approval of others.

Now, approval is a thing frequently desired, and it can be graciously accepted when offered. But the gracious acceptance of approval was something that I could not do in the past. Accepting approval is the fruition of the Bible verse in which Jesus said, "Love others as you love yourself." Like many other preachers of the Word, I used that verse often but majored on the "Love others" part, forgetting or ignoring the "as you love yourself" bit. Like the song says, "Ya can't have one without the other." In fact, self denial had been so ingrained in me by my succumbing to those messages of denying self, that it would have been a sin for me to have loved myself.

An extreme example of this took place in the Baptist church which influenced my life so much as a child. I am not even sure if it was from scripture, but the pastor had a verse printed on a piece of paper glued into each hymnal in the church. On it was written, "I was born in iniquity, and in sin did my mother conceive me." My god! Can you imagine what that did to each of us as we read it out loud every Sunday? I know what it did to me. Some did not read it. Some did not accept it. But some, like me, again took it like a fish, hook, line and sinker. That was NOT the way to create good self esteem.

Everything in my early life directed me not to love myself, but instead to despise totally who I was. The church was just part of it, but I chose to make everything a part of it. I had to be somewhat of a recluse if I believed that I was worthless, and I did not want to expose others to my negativity. I didn't comprehend my behavior at the time, but in retrospect I now understand it. I did not even have a date until I was a senior in college, and then the girl had to ask me. I seldom played with other kids, seeking out only those companions that most of my classmates considered unimportant, low class individuals. Perhaps I sensed a comradeship there with like suffering souls. After all, I COULD feel their pain.

I was the perfect kid in that sense, doing what I was told to do, trying to win everyone's approval, while at the same time, not being able to accept that approval.

It is very unlikely that one can accept approval if one does not approve of self. Perhaps one could learn to find self approval if they were in a long term relationship where "approval energy" (new term for me) was constantly provided. After all, is that not what a family should be all about? Shouldn't a child expect to be loved, not only by what is verbally stated by the parents but by the very energy that is always there. It seems very obvious to me that a child "feels" the loving energy of a parent, even more so than the spoken word. Even now, when Pattie is disturbed about something, I can sense that, even if she says nothing. If she is joyful, I can also sense that.

So, why did Pattie and I get married? I hope this makes some sense, because it only barely does to me. If one accepts the concept that most of what we do is from subconscious motivation, then it makes sense to think that self denial, poor self esteem, and the absence of self love were the motivating factors of my entire life until age sixty-two. Why then, would it not be my motivation for finding a marriage partner as well?

I never felt worthy enough to ask a girl for a date. Nor did I feel adequate enough to present myself as someone to be admired, loved, accepted or respected. As a teenager, I was frequently asked for dates and earlier was praised for being such a "wonderful" child. I rejected those advances and compliments with the thought, "But you just don't know how bad I am."

So why did I accept Pattie's offer for a date to see the opera Aida while I was a student at Oklahoma Baptist University? Perhaps I was giving in to a desire to have someone care for me, finally waking up to that need. Or maybe I was just too frugal to buy my own ticket to see an opera for the first time. I do believe that since I had known Pattie most of my life, and saw how she was different from others, I felt I might be safe with her. *

When I say that I felt "safe with her" I am speaking from that subconscious part of me of which I am most aware at this writing. Or to put it succinctly, "I set myself up for what I thought I deserved." And yes, I believe that is what most humans do. I am not judging them; it's just what I have observed in people's behavior over the past seventy-four years.

The "sinful" sexual part of me did not deserve to be satisfied, so I would marry someone whom I felt would not call upon that part of me to be expressed. Of course, that doesn't work because the sexual drive is a powerful one that does not want to be deprived of the experience. Are you with me?

   *Pattie and I talked about including this section in the book because I felt that if it were not included, the main theme of the book would be missed – that of unwisely trying to be what one thinks other people want them to be. So, if you are reading this, you will know that she concurred.

I was setting myself up to fail, which is what I believed I deserved in my subconscious. That is why "workaholism" is such a self destructive process. Constant approval is needed but cannot be received because the person does not even approve of self. It is no more possible to do this than to fulfill the

61

admonition by Jesus to "Love others as you love yourself." Or, as the modern Psychic Children say, as spoken of by James Twyman, "Let the Beloved see the Beloved." If we don't see or know loveliness within self, then we cannot see it in others. We will not even know what we are trying to see.

Until my self re-creation in November of 1991, I tried to change Pattie to be what I wanted her to be, "for me." I could not have handled the change even if she had been able to do so. A part of me finally realized that if any change were to occur, it had to be from within myself and not in those around me. This great struggle between us went on for years, and I hurt her many times with my disapproval of who she was even though I spoke of my love for her. I did not physically abuse her but did a greater harm with emotional abuse. Yet, she tolerated it. Perhaps it was her own way of setting herself up with what she felt she deserved in life. But that is for her to determine.

Was it a "bad" thing? I think not. Had it been otherwise, had she changed to be what she thought that I wanted her to be, it would have been a disaster and brought greater harm than was already there. She was not a threat to me by trying to give me that which I could not receive. Nor was I a threat to her in trying to give to her what she could not receive.

I could not receive what I desired the most, and she could not give in the way that I thought was giving. And, somehow, that brought some type of strange comfort to both of us. That is why it was so important for me to hear Pattie say, as I left for the first trip to Esalen, "Jim, I know you need to do this, and I know you may not come back. And that is okay." That is why it was so important, that when I did come back, she started sharing her self with me because I was now able to honor who she was, as she honored me.

I must mention here that my brother, who was four years my elder and raised in the same sexually dysfunctional family that I was, had his own way of trying to find peace of mind and happiness. Carrying the "someone out there to make me happy" theme a bit further, he married four times as he repeatedly kept trying to find the "right" one. I am not judging him as "right" or "wrong." I am just observing his way of living his own Earth journey.

My deepest feeling concerning this matter is that no one or nothing "out there" will bring the peace of mind that we desire. It only comes from within. It reminds me of something I used to preach in fear, paraphrasing of course, "Neither life nor death, things present nor things to come, height or depth, kings or principalities, can separate us from the love of God." And, if my feeling is correct that God "became" all that is, including sentient beings, then that would mean I cannot separate myself from my own love. That would translate into, "Nothing outside of me can determine who I am." I will always be this particular soul, this vibration, this music, throughout my existence. I will evolve as I choose to evolve. And that is a pretty grand and spectacular thing, isn't it?

Sometimes, this long term positive relationship of marriage or companionship is called psychotherapy in which the ideal therapist represents that consistency of love no matter what the person reveals to them. Are we not seeking love when we seek that sort of help from others? My therapist accepted me, at least in my mind, even though I did not accept myself as I flooded her with tales of my perceived failures as a human being. She did not cast me out. Had she done so, I would have been back to "square one" or perhaps even worse.

To be honest, I would not want to be in the shoes of any psychotherapist. While I was healing, it was essential for me to be in a place of total and unconditional acceptance. That is why it is so easy to "fall in love" with one's therapist. It is so difficult in that state to accept one's own loveliness, so it is almost automatic that the client project that love onto the therapist, thinking that it must be from her or him.

The obviousness of that concept became apparent to me when I conducted a drum workshop in Lake City, a most beautiful, small mountain hamlet in southwest Colorado. We drummed in an old theater and had ten participants, one being a Native American lady. I felt deeply honored that she attended and learned much from her. One of the potential drummers was a somewhat rugged but pretty young lady in her late twenties.

63

She was deep in the throes of depression because of her lover's recent departure. Not a good way to bolster self esteem I thought.

When I conduct a drum workshop, I try to be open and "feel" what each person needs so that I may better serve them. That is not always possible, especially if there are those present with much negative energy. However, in this case, I was clearly guided by "an inner force" that urged me to have this young lady use a drum I had personally made. It was a wonderful drum, and had a water buffalo head, a very low sounding skin.

I had her place her hands flat on the drum, close her eyes and "see" herself in Africa standing next to the skin donor. Her hands were on the female buffalo's side and she could feel the rippling muscles sending her energy. As she continued with her visioning, the buffalo turned its head and gave permission to use her skin for such a purpose, and to thank us for honoring her spirit.

Becky, we shall call her, drummed as if she had been drumming for years, amazing herself as well as the rest of us. About half way through the session, Becky jumped up from her chair, looked at me and said loudly, "I love you!" Whoa! I was not ready for that, but it became clear what was happening. Just like in the office of the psychotherapist, the client was unable to accept the love of self that was being generated and projected it to the teacher. I almost laughed in relief as the realization took hold within me.

Becky wanted a private lesson, and while I almost tried to sexualize that, I knew that I had to place myself in the position of healer instead of that of a conquistador. Trying to help with her healing, I knew I was still working on my own. We went to the small cabin that she was house sitting and drummed like children, laughing and crying. And like the old saying goes, "A good time was had by all."

As I was starting to leave, she became worried that she would not continue in her present state without a drum. So, I gave her one. That is what I do, sometimes selling them, sometimes giving them away when appropriate. Having learned more about following my intuition, I had earlier loaded up an extra drum when leaving for Colorado, a drum that I did not particularly like but others did. And right before me was the reason for that action. It was so Becky could have a drum of her own. I later heard through a friend of hers that her life had changed for the better, and that she had since gotten married.

Like many others who seek counseling, I fell "in love" with my psychotherapist, Francis. I "wanted her" and in my imagination saw myself running off with her, living happily ever after. Pattie was aware of my obsession, but said nothing. As is her beautiful way, she let me work through my issues. She did that a lot. The matter of my attachment to my therapist became acute when her husband divorced her and the announcement of the divorce was listed in the local newspaper. I later learned from Pattie that when she saw the divorce listing in the newspaper, she felt our marriage was over and I would be leaving to run off with Francis. But, I didn't do that. Whether it was my Christian upbringing, a sense of loyalty, or perhaps my Higher Self telling me that I needed Pattie more than I knew at this time of life, I managed to keep a cool head.

I like to call the love that I felt I had for Francis, a dependent love, one that continuously fed me the acceptance that I had not been able to give to myself. I could only hope that this would turn into a non-dependent love and felt that "this too would pass." That was a phrase that was often spoken by one of my Radiology associates and one which irritated the hell out of me. But, how right he was.

This "idealized" love remained present for some time after finishing my official tenure with Francis, and culminated with a bitter sweet experience at the *Creativity and Madness Conference* in Santa Fe, New Mexico. It was a fine week long conference, mostly for psychotherapists and "wanna-be" healers like me. And, it was a good way for me to legitimately see Francis, which seemed no problem for Pattie, as she encouraged me to see and communicate with Francis

65

frequently. I am thinking as I write this, "Thank you, Jesus" for such a patient, long suffering companion.

I had expressed to another psychologist attending the conference that I felt I was at a place in life of self approval; that I no longer needed the attention and support offered by Francis. A bold statement, as I was soon to learn.

The first morning of the conference Francis and I sat together, and at the end of the day gave our, "See you tomorrow" goodbyes. The next day, I looked for her but unable to find her, assumed she had not come. Sitting a bit closer to the stage than usual, I would occasionally glance to the rear to see if she had arrived. Various emotions were raging within me from, "She is sitting with someone else today. Perhaps she is avoiding me." to, "Maybe she is very ill." After the final conference lecture that day, I got up and turned to leave. Many individuals had already gone and a clear pathway was open to where Francis and I usually sat. There she was, sitting and talking to another guy. "Well! Wonder what that is about?" I thought, as my mind went racing.

Thinking that it might be better to just leave and not acknowledge her, I tried to do that, but finally decided it would be better to face her and see what was going on. I approached within ten feet and she seemed to be looking right at me but not seeing me. I said something, not loudly, and she did not seem to hear, still talking to the other guy. I almost laughed when the thought came to me, "knowing" that it was correct, "This is a test! A self made test to see if I really am at a place in life where I no longer need her approval."

I had said to myself earlier in the day that even if she told me that I was crazy, stupid, sinful and hopeless, it would make no difference. That would be her problem, not mine. So, this great feeling of success and fulfillment came over me as I realized what was happening; VAS DER PLAN, my plan. I passed with flying colors knowing that I had seemingly been rejected and did not decompensate. Francis seemed to get as big a kick out of it as I did when I told her the next day.

What had happened? My dependent love had turned into an independent love. I still loved her, but I no longer had to have the love she had shown to me in order to be who I am. I did not have to "possess" her to be loved, as I had been taught or was conditioned to think in childhood, "To be loved, one has to have sex. But sex is a sin."

The issue of self esteem is so important, yet it is something most of us pay little attention to or understand clearly. As a child, I felt a constant loneliness, so I did those things that lonely people do. At school, during recess, I would go off by myself. I would watch the girls playing house, drawing the outline of a house in the dirt, all the while wanting to be a part of that family. I was not a wimp, even though I kept to myself most of the time. I did play "spike the marbles" a lot, a way of gambling for marbles, as was playing "for keeps." Can you believe that I actually felt that I was sinning? I can't believe it either. There were the occasional bullies with whom to contend, and I did that very well. One good poke was usually all that was needed, so they left me alone.

I would often sit on the front porch absorbed in the misery of my loneliness, unaware that others could see that I was miserable. Pattie's mother used to drive by on the way into town from their farm, see me alone on the porch and would feel a deep ache, sharing my loneliness, knowing some of my family's problems even though I did not.

I did get into a fight once with our preacher's son; I think his last name was Smith. My folks were not at home, and this kid and I were duking it out. I was on the bottom, getting the worst of it. Suddenly, I saw my parents' car and knew they were almost home. That inspired me to great feats of strength, and I quickly flipped this kid over and was on top, whaling the daylights out of him. Do you suppose that had something to do with wanting to make my parents proud of me, but in a fairly negative way? You are probably right. I think that I got chastened instead of praised. Sort of like your cat presenting you with a dead mouse in its mouth. That would be a high compliment, but it is rarely perceived as such.

Sometimes after elementary school let out, I would make my way back to the school grounds. The school building was only a block away from our house. I would go to the shrubbery like trees in the creek on the East side of the playground. I had fashioned a sort of nest-like place in the top of one where I could be secluded. Hmmm. Wonder if this has a connection with my Sea Gull rebirthing? Frequently, I would take a mayonnaise sandwich, along with a Boy Scout canteen containing Kool Aid. There I would do my day dreaming about life, sometimes good, sometimes bad. There usually was a bit of crying, in self pity.

You would think one would lose the lonely feeling while at school. I imagine there are many who feel lonely in a crowd, like I did. What I wanted was there for me, but when it was offered, was turned away. A girl once told me that she felt I was saying to her, but not with my voice, "Come here." and as she approached, would get the opposite message, "Go away." Such is the life of a person who does not think he or she is lovely enough to be loved but desperately desires that love. It is the constant looking elsewhere for something that is only found within. No one can bring us happiness but ourselves. We have not been taught correctly. We are constantly told to look here and look there for success, happiness, for the one person God has for us. As long as we fix our gaze on what is outside of us as most important, then we will never accept the beauty within. I did not come to Earth to live the journey of someone else. I came to live my own. I did not come to Earth to be like Jesus. I came to be like Jim. Of course I can learn from Jesus and others the best way to live that life and find my true self. What did He say? "I did not come to judge the world but that the world through what I am saying and living might have life, and life more abundantly." Is that a paraphrase or did he really mean that? Perhaps that is what is meant by working out our own salvation. How many times have the sayings of Jesus been changed to fit what the changer wanted Him to say? Did not King James do that? And to a greater extent Popes Constantine and Clement? Yes. They did. Who are we to believe, a stranger who tells us he has our truth, or shall we believe our own hearts and the evidence of the Universe around us which speaks of the majesty of God, Light, Universe, Creator, etc.

Are we not the magnificence of God, expressed? How does God reveal Herself other than by Her creations and co-creations? Are we not the mirrors through which the All sees Itself and is able to say, "It is very good"? Okay, okay. Here we go. I'm on a roll. It is time for the Big Kahuna, to talk about the secret of life. Want to know that? So do I.

Do you remember the womb thing earlier in this essay, where I hung on so desperately to keep from coming into the world that I tore my mother's uterus? It took me six years following that incident to get to the place where I could freely consider who I was. The revelation concerning my own identity took place while I was standing in the yard at 405 North Grant Street. Suddenly, I just knew that I was part of God – a cell in this giant holy Being and not separate at all, beautiful in all aspects. I must have told my parents or someone about this and remember being told to get rid of that kind of thinking or I would go to hell. Sort of like when my mother caught me masturbating, and I was told to stop that kind of behavior or I would go crazy. Of course I didn't quit, but I sure felt guilty about it each time I did it. And, believe it or not, hair didn't grow on my palm. But you will have to ask someone else about the crazy part.

Well, that was certainly short lived – the sudden, intense and so brief understanding of the secret of life. After my parental "censorship," I decided I wouldn't talk about it to anybody, for sure. I was easily convinced that I was created by a loving God who would send me to hell if I didn't do what He said to do. It was a "free choice" they told me. I just had to be sure I made the right choice or goodbye Jimmy. It seems so absurd now that I would buy into that. So, I went from loving God and being part of God, to thinking I was only loved if I behaved a certain way, and would be sent to hell if I didn't. That is probably why I was such a "good" kid, nauseatingly good.

How many time have we heard this quoted from the Christian Bible, "Bring up a child in the way he should go and he will not depart from it?" Or, in other words, be sure the kid believes like you do and does not make his or her own choices in life. Constantly make him feel guilty so he will be afraid to travel his own journey. Of course, each child DOES have the right and CAN make those decisions, but I did not realize that and took the easy way out, being what I was told to be. I went along with the lie, "Don't expect anything and you will not be disappointed."

My brother and I always seemed to be at odds with each other. He chose one way in life, and I chose another. And, in my opinion, we were both wrong. But we will visit that being "right" or "wrong" again later in this story. He probably will think that I do not love him because of what I am saying but that is far from the truth. I have found that I can love all, honor all journeys but that does not mean that I agree with them or that I am comfortable in their presence. Is that begging the question? When I am strong enough in my own self, perhaps it will not matter when I am around those with what I consider negative energy. I love the saying of a Qigong Master who says "There is neither good energy nor bad energy. There is just energy, until we perceive it otherwise." As I write this line, I am feeling a yearning to again visit my brother to share in love the Earthly connection that we have.

10

THE LESSONS CONTINUE

My first love was Alma Lee, two classes ahead of me in high school. The "head over heels" thing happened in study hall where kids used to spend their out of class time, presumably studying. I actually did study, knowing that someone was watching me all the time to be sure I was a good boy. Alma was two seats to my left.

During study hall one day I was having trouble reading. I had glasses since the age of six. Alma noticed my difficulty and said, "Give me your glasses." Hey, I do what I am told. I gave them to her and she meticulously cleaned them and handed them back. I was awestruck. Someone actually gave me something. Someone actually knew I was alive and cared for me. So much for studying the rest of that hour.

My fantasies ran rampant for the next few days, and Alma was all I could think about. I finally wrote a nervous note of my eternal love with a request for her to be my girlfriend. One evening, I stealthily delivered it to her mailbox, trying to keep the old wooden floor of the porch from creaking and giving me away.

It was an emotional hell for me waiting for her answer that I did not expect to come. I was terrified that she would say, "Yes Jimmy, I love you and want to be with you always." I wouldn't know what to do. I wasn't smart enough to talk to a girl. I was too young to drive. I had never even asked a girl for a date. I hoped she would say no, but I also knew that it would be such a hurt. It would be yet another rejection, but that is the way it should be I thought. I was more fearful that she would not reject me. As it turned out, she did reject me, but she did it in such a nice and understanding way. She had a boyfriend, and although she admired me, was not free to date another. Whew! I got out of that one.

People did not treat my mother very well for some reason, especially my Dad. It wasn't until my fifties that I found out the reason. Prior to my being "saved" at the age of twelve, my parents were party people, frequently having drunken parties at the house until the wee hours of the morning. The house would reek with cigar and cigarette smoke and one time a couple, not married, came into our bedroom (my brother and I shared a common bed) sat on the bed next to me and made out. Not sex but just heavy smooching as we called it. I did not like that. My space had been violated.

Dad was a classic workaholic, a productive one, and was not able to really share with me or my brother. He did like to fish though and would get me up very early in the morning to go with him to the lake. He had me row the simple little metal fishing boat while he trolled for fish. I really hated that. If he were at home working on something, he could not tolerate any help or questions, so it was much easier just to leave him alone. Dad was a good poker player however and partially kept us in food during the Great Depression of 1929 with his winnings. His work as a pharmacist in his Rexall Drug store did not bring in enough to support us.

The folks would frequently go dancing at night clubs in those days, and I figured every kid's mother and father did that. It did hit home a bit when they could not get a baby sitter one Friday evening and took me with them to a dance hall in Clinton, fifteen miles away. I was left in the back seat to amuse myself while they danced and drank for several hours, or so it seemed. I did not like that but I thought it was better not to complain. I had visions of the razor strap when correcting needed to be done. Just the thought of it made me want to stay in line and not agitate anyone.

I do remember one time when I was in bed with the flu and they were planning on going dancing even though I did not have anyone to stay with me. I was old enough then to be by myself, but a sick kid does like to have his mother around at times like that. I was crushed when they left me alone, all the while begging them to stay. Perhaps we see our childhood as we want to see it.

Of course, I knew my parents loved me when my father bought me a brand new set of unfinished bedroom furniture, including a wonderful study desk. I could not believe it and was in hog heaven as they say. About a week later, Dad decided we really could not afford it and returned it to the store. There must have been a logical reason for his behavior, but as far as I was concerned, this was the ultimate rejection, confirming my unworthiness. Oh yes, there were plenty of confirmations of that.

My mother spent most of her time working at the drugstore, selling cosmetics. I would get myself up early in the morning in order to get ready for school, and then spend what time was left on the dining room floor listening to my little square Motorola radio. It was an old fashioned radio with a wet battery that could not be tipped too much or it would spill. It was square, deep purple, and I held it close like one would do with a pet. I never had a pet. Think about that. After that it was off to school, about a mile away, without breakfast. I did not know that the other kids ate breakfast until an assignment in Science class required us to list what we ate each day. I think it was a way to find out who needed food as well as to alert school officials if we were not being adequately fed.

I was incensed, embarrassed and just all around pissed off when I found out that all the other kids ate breakfast, even the poor kid on the block, so to speak. I don't think I got half the calories he got in one day, or even in a week. Here I was, not eating breakfast, coming home at noon for lunch and having a mayonnaise sandwich (which I loved) and returning to school. Many times I remember sitting there; eating that white bread sandwich, sobbing and wishing someone were there with me. Shoot, if I had eaten properly, I might have grown up with some smarts. I am sure that a lot of this is how I remember it to be, and most likely it was not as bad as it seems. Yes, I know. Denial is not a river in Egypt or, I may just be trying to justify my parents' actions or their lack of them. Sometimes, a child is just not loved. That is the way it is. If my mother ever told me that she did love me, it does not erase the vision I have as a little baby looking up into what I perceived as cold, uncaring eyes.

It should be said somewhere in this essay that this is not my way of finding fault with others, blaming them for my choices in life, or holding them accountable for the way I have lived my journey. I take full responsibility, for that is the way I had it planned. Many will not accept that idea, and that is okay. I am not trying to convince anyone to think as I think or believe as I believe, because I might change some beliefs as the days pass, and hopefully I will gain some wisdom and discernment along the way.

At the moment, I like to think that we were in spirit before we decided to come to Earth to live in a human body. It also seems reasonable to think that there are spirit groups that plan on how they will spend life after life, perhaps trading out different roles so that the more experiences one has in the body, the faster one will evolve spiritually. It works better for me believing that way than the way I was brought up to believe; that I had a chance to go to Heaven and even a better chance of going to hell. One place created for suffering and another to sit around forever and do what?

What that would mean then is that no matter what my experiences in life, they are neither good nor bad, but just experiences by which I evolve. It is very difficult to get out of the judgment stage and to honor the journeys of all, whatever they are. How boring it would be if we all agreed. It would also mean that what might seem a very bad thing, like a young child dying, a war, or even the destruction of the World Trade Center on September 11 with the loss of so many lives, could serve a very important purpose in all of the lives that were lost.

Someone recently asked me why a two year old had to die. Why did God let that happen? It is possible that because of that young child's passing, many wonderful things happened to those who knew her and many reconciliations were possible which otherwise may not have been. It is very difficult for some to think that she might have planned it this way in the "before life" to fulfill her own destiny. That would mean that there are no "good" and no "bad" events in life, but just experiences by which we grow into our greater state of existence, an existence which is without beginning or ending. That has to be my opinion, of course, because I surely can't prove it.

While living on North Grant Street, my brother and I shared a tiny room that had a small dresser and one chest of drawers. There may have been a tiny closet, but I am not sure about that. The walls were painted a sickly light green color, sort of like vomit. That was its effect on me. The old iron bedstead, with paint peeling off its parts, was very narrow so when someone wet the bed, I could just barely escape the urine as it crept toward me.

The head of the bed was against the west wall and above it was a copy of a famous painting, *The End of the Trail*. The painting depicted a scene of a Native American, slumped on his horse, while holding his spear. He was looking out over the Pacific Ocean with no more land for him to escape to in order to get away from the white man. That is the way I felt most of my early youth as I identified with him. It was sort of like I was hanging over the edge of the bed, trying to escape the wetness.

In those days, it was not uncommon for young country girls, just out of high school, to live in homes to do housework, cook and take care of the children. We had several such helpers over the years, one at a time. I am sure mother thought this impressed her bridge club. I have to tell you this for it reminds me of an incident which involved the "very proper" bridge club.

It was my mother's day to host them at our house, and they were busy doing whatever one does while playing bridge. My brother and I were playing outside. He told me something that I just could not believe, and encouraged me to go ask our mother if it were true or not. I ran into the house, stopped beside mother, and as everyone looked at me, said, "Mother, Sammy says that mountain oysters are bull nuts. Is that true?" There may have been some embarrassment on my mother's part, and I think that I left hurriedly. In fact, I think I was even encouraged to do so.

When we did have a housekeeper, she would stay in the room next to ours. I do not remember if anything went on sexually with any of them as far as Sam and I were concerned. But I would not be surprised if something did, even though I cannot remember being sexually abused. I got that story from Sam who said we were abused at the same time, when he was about nine. I have evidently wiped it from my memory, and even with hypnotism can not recall it. No matter. My therapist said if anyone ever was abused, I certainly had the personality that would indicate that it had happened.

There is no joy in talking about my family like this, but that is where life is, the nitty gritty of it, the reactions to the experiences in my daily living, and the choices that I made to survive. To be able to think in retrospect, after having learned how to be insightful, is a blessing I never thought to have, and I thank myself for letting me do so.

To see how I survived "life" so that others might see similarities in their own lives and KNOW that they too have the right to be who they really are, is the reason for my writing this book. If I could not expose myself, so to speak, and the input of others close to me, there would be no book to write. Who would want to hear, "I suffered more than you did, ha ha!" The victory is in learning how to handle that suffering, if indeed that is what it is. It makes life so exciting and existence in the eternal flow of the Universe that it just blows me away. Someone must have said, "Out of darkness comes Light." How many lifetimes does it take to get there? No, that is not a joke question. It is a serious concept worth considering. We might actually live many lives in order to have the experience of being a human being, to help us, and the rest of the Universe, evolve. So many individuals, particularly in organized religions, are afraid of change, as I was and as my parents were their entire lives. To me, life is change and that is its purpose and shall always be. I have to believe that we are consciousness, eternal energy, and when something changes in each of us it is felt by the consciousness of the Universe. Perhaps that is what is meant by the Bible verse, paraphrasing, and "A bird cannot fall without God knowing it." Perhaps the Collective Consciousness of the Universe IS God.

I quote Jesus a lot because he is the only Ascended Master that I know personally. He also said, "Nothing has visited you that is not common to all." Wow! Could that mean that each human being goes through the same hell on Earth? About three years ago, I was delighted to read a statement concerning the Catholic Pope. In the newspaper article, someone asked the Pope about hell. His answer was, and I have the clip from the paper, "Hell is not a reality. It is a state of mind." One cannot say that this one suffers more than that one. Some would want to be better than others even if it is to be better at suffering. Geez!

It was quite obvious in the medical profession and in the ministry that many enjoyed the failure of others, that being their only claim to fame. Living off the failure of others is some form of competition but it is not a healthy concept. That is why it is such a joy to teach African hand drumming the way that I do, in a non-judgmental and non-competitive way. When I teach a student, I want them to be better than I am, to enjoy it more than I do. What does it profit me to want others to be less than I? Didn't the Apostles of Jesus get into the same mess? He kept telling them that he came to show us a spiritual kingdom and not a physical one. Even his two most prominent apostles, John and Peter, argued about which one of them would be at the right hand of Christ when in Heaven. Jesus had the message. They did not hear it. He was responsible for the message but neither for the way it was received nor the way it was used.

It has been fascinating to observe that we each see, hear and perceive all of the other human sensations from our context of life. We certainly can't perceive it from the context of the life of another, can we? So, if I tell two people all this stuff I am saying, that I think is so important, will either of them receive it the same way or act on it the same way? Don't bet on it. They won't even be able to describe what this handsome old man looks like, the same way. We are very judgmental in all that we do if we are not free from seeking approval and have not approved of self. If we judge ourselves to be unworthy, then we will seek to overcome that false perception by seeing the "bad" or unworthiness in everybody else. There is no end to that and therefore no progress in accepting the beauty of who we are, who we have always been, and who we will always be. That is what we are to remember, according to the Psychic Children. Oh, my goodness. Who are they? Stay tuned. We will keep you advised.

When a small child, I was sure that I was in the wrong family, a common feeling according to psychotherapists. "Surely these people were not my parents," I thought. My brother even kidded me about being a Jew, since I have a large nose. Sure, I took that on just like I did when anyone told me how bad I was. Surely they would not lie about that. The curious thing is that I felt like I was Jewish, so much so that I used to spend time with the only Jewish family in town and with their son. I felt at home there. They lived next door to my first grade teacher, the world's best teacher, Mrs. Dodson.

Now, I was not consciously aware of my parents' "activities" before my birth. It seems, however, everybody else in town was, including Pattie. The revelations about my parents' history became known to me when my Dad died in 1987.

A short time before that, when I visited him in the hospital, his two main concerns still seemed to be obsessions with sex and money; I am not sure in what order. He was slightly sitting up in bed attempting to talk, in a muffled voice. He had a nasogastric tube in place, so I asked for the X-Ray of his abdomen. There was no sign of the tube being where it should be. It was coiled in the back of his throat where it had been for several days. I was very angry at the poor care he was receiving even though it did not seem to be bothering him. I am telling you this to show you where Dad was. When a nurse would come in, Dad would start flirting with her with the usual little quips that have two meanings, and here he was, dying!

When he did die, my brother came to me and told me Dad had just passed away. The next statement he made threw me into a tailspin. He remembers it somewhat differently as far as the situation but does remember saying, "We are not sure you are Dad's son." My God! What did he just say? I did not even ask why he said it, or for proof, or respond with any sane question. I just accepted his remarks as true, since at that time in my life, my nature was to be whatever I was told to be. I didn't even have the presence of mind to think that he might have said it to hurt me, which I think is most likely. I had not asked him why he said that until just recently. His answer was that he had found out it was not true anyway, but failed to tell me that, leaving me in that tailspin into hell and my subsequent discovery of court records of the sordid story about my mother and the traveling salesman.

That is the way it was with us. My brother was the successful Eagle Scout, and I did not even have hair on my legs when I boarded the train to go to Philmont Scout Ranch in New Mexico. Sam was gregarious, hairy, and extroverted and easily put me down because I would take it so well. He was the one whose picture I left out in the drawing of my family the first time I was at Esalen. You will not be surprised when I tell you that I finally had to divorce myself from his negative attitude. On attempting a reconciliation meeting a few years ago, his opening remark was "You sure did hurt Dad." When I asked how, he replied, "Well, once Dad asked you how much you made a month as a physician and you would not tell him." I could not believe this was his first greeting to me. It was obvious it would not work, so I left.

This "not my father's son" bit started me on a long, scary journey that had a delightful ending. My mother, still living, was not to escape the effect of that statement on me. I started asking questions. One of the first sources of inquiry was my oldest living relative, Aunt Mae, who assured me that I WAS my Dad's son. Yes, the "Dad" of her story, my Dad, was Sam Arnold, Sr.

As I learned the rest of the story, it all started to make sense. Now I could begin to understand how my mother was treated by some in the small farming community, and how I was treated as well. While I had never heard the story of my suspicious birth, the energy of it had been well known to me as I always felt I was in the wrong home, and that my true parents must be Jewish.

You won't believe this, or maybe you will.

THE RED BUICK

My Dad's red Buick brought them together
Erotic farm girl you could not tether
A fatherless son whose love was mechanics
Pharmacy was forced, no time for romantics.

Workaholic was he, paying little attention
Lonely was she, left to her own invention
A traveling salesman, yes, this is the story
A two day tryst brought her little glory

Caught by the cops, thrown into jail
The law said prison, there only to wail
An OUT was then given, if she would consent
To confess to the church and really repent

Ah, mother, sweet mother, what agony and fear
To tear out your soul for judges to hear.
He would keep her, with one more stipulation
Sex as he wanted, the final degradation.

To find the motivation for the poem was my task after being told I was a bastard. Aunt Mae continued. Dad and his mother, a very proper fundamentalist and intelligent lady, had bought the local Rexall Drug Store. I was fortunate to have two grandmothers, Grandmother Kerley being Dad's mother. My Dad's father had died before he was born. Alma Kerley was a hardy soul, not tall, but large and firm. She walked with authority and, and seemed to have usurped the personalities of my Dad and his two step brothers, Junior and Arthur.

When I visited her as a child, I sat in a very sturdy, straight backed oak chair and felt like an Army private being interrogated by his Sergeant. She was not mean, just strong, and her energy spoke to that. It is no surprise to me that Dad would take the less calamitous choice of doing what his mother wanted him to do. He wanted to be a mechanic, but that was not to be. She wanted him to be a pharmacist and a pharmacist he was, hating it all of his life. He was such a natural at working with boat and automobile engines, even though they often ran less smoothly following his manipulations. Every outboard motor he would buy for his boat sounded "faulty" and he would immediately commence to fix it. My grand children have that same trait, to tear something apart to see how it works, never thinking about how to put it together.

He was very good however, making Indian bows of Bois de arc posts which he would buy off trucks coming through. He deftly used the draw knife as he took away the wood that did not look or feel like a bow. I admired him for that and longed to have that touch.

My other grandmother was Grandmother Lillie, or Lillie Belle to be formal. She was a wiry little farm wife whose struggles in the dust of Oklahoma to "make do" for her family were clearly shown on her face. She was the "rascal" and it finally dawned on me that was what mother chose to be. She was little like a child, and mischievous like a child with a slightly "dirty" mind. Her husband, Mom's Dad, Bill Richmond was a large, strong and handsome man. I don't think that he drove a red Buick. I remember once, out of the blue when he told me he didn't think God Himself could please that woman (my grandmother). I did not know what he meant then, but I do now.

When Grandmother Kerley and Dad opened the drug store, it took all of their time, and unfortunately more than they should have given it. It was a struggle to survive, just before the Great Depression of 1929. I totally understand Dad's being a workaholic for I was chief among the workaholics (as the Apostle Paul might say) and knew of the abnormal drive to "succeed" and the inability to accept success when gained. Dad and Mom could not afford their own house. As there were no apartments available, they lived about 19 miles away in Sentinel, Oklahoma with Aunt Mae and her husband Alvin McKerley, an insurance salesman. Dad was at work most of the time and mother was home, wanting some action. She found some with a Jewish traveling clothing salesman (yes, you heard me correctly) who frequented The Dixie Store a block to the East of the Rexall Drug store. My mother worked there some and so a natural meeting of the two occurred. And, I hope this will make the story a bit more interesting for you, my wife's mother worked at that store; and yes, that is how she knew a great deal of the story.

Was it a setup meant to fail? You betcha! It was a dalliance waiting to happen. Seems that mother was taken with this salesman, and he was taken with her. But he should not have taken her for a ride a few miles North on a dirt road near Bessie, Oklahoma to have their affair.

Somehow Dad found out about their "road trip." (I wish I knew how he did, but everybody is dead now that would know.) He had grabbed a gun, and was on his way to kill one or both of them. Would this make a good book or what? Fortunately for all, it was a dark and stormy night and Dad got stuck on the muddy dirt road. He returned to Cordell and got the Sheriff to do his duty. The salesman was soon in jail since adultery was a crime, not just a sin, punishable by up to 5 years in prison. Still is. I had my very organized daughter-in-law, Shari, search the Washita County records to see if the facts were there. They were.

Grandmother talked Dad into demanding that if mother would confess her sins before the local church, repent and do what he told her to do the rest of his life, including sexual activity, he would take her back and not press charges on the poor soul rotting in the county jail. It is difficult for me to believe that she accepted, but she did and made the confession in front of the little town's Baptist congregation with her mother at her side. As the story was told to me, Grandmother Lillie patted her on the shoulder and said, "Its okay honey. We all have to go through this." I don't want to hear the reason for that statement, but I will tell you that Mom and Dad punished each other for the rest of their lives.

I always knew something was wrong without knowing what it was. Everyone in Cordell knew it but Sam and me. Can you believe that? It is true. The only place we seemed to function as a family was when we went to Southwest Colorado on vacations, to fish. When Dad bought a little house in Creede, we would spend a couple of weeks there each year.

How different we were. We would fish together, hike together, eat together and have the most fun playing cards, dominos and Yahtzee, laughing until we could hardly breathe. When we returned home, all that changed and it was mostly negative.

I could not understand why Dad gave mother so little money to run the house, and why she did not complain. I did not understand why he spent so much time at the drugstore. Piecing together information from various sources, including my parents, the following is the gist of how they would use sex, or the withholding of sex, to punish each other. Since mother agreed to have sex any time Dad wanted it, it would usually be when they were in bed. She would be on her side while he had sex, while she countered by going to sleep. And so it went on throughout the years.

Now, why on Earth would I put such a personal story in this book? BECAUSE, it is time that we admit what we have done in living this life that has been given to us. To ADMIT how we have mismanaged it and to show what humans actually do to one another. It is time to quit pretending that all is well in our families (unless it is) so that we can awaken to our own true identity. I am not relating these stories in order to embarrass anyone, but to show how we can arise from the ashes, so to speak, like the Phoenix.

While touched on previously, I want to stress the way humans use a beautiful act of sexual union as a negative quantity in order to control and/or punish those with whom they share it or withhold it. This negativism pervades all cultures, especially those with fundamentalist religions, as the act of sex is somehow so vile that it is not conceivable that Jesus could have been produced by a human sexual union, much less having partaken of it himself. To be who he came to be must necessitate celibacy, even as Paul, the Apostle said "It is better to be as I am" which has been interpreted by many as being celibate.

A child may react in horror upon discovering that his or her parents actually "did it" and hopefully will never have to actually witness the doing of it. It is a common saying, when speaking of parents and sex to hear "Not my parents!" And yet, sex is touted at the ultimate expression of sharing to be saved for what is called legal or holy matrimony (wedlock). Sex may be seen as the ultimate expression of love or used as the ultimate method of debasement and control of both women and men. The intent of the one seeking control may say "I will take from you that which you and I value most in life."

Ah yes. The ultimate dichotomy.

I must tell you again that even though what I am writing might make you think that I do not love my family, I do, even more so now that I have a better understanding of life.

It is so easy to forget, or to be unaware of, what is transpiring during our Earth journeys. We are so ready to repress, to deny. Some individuals even go out of body when the perception of being abused is there, choosing to repress those events, which then subtly, or not so subtly, affect them the rest of their lives. Each person must decide what to do with these experiences since we cannot take the journey of another. I am not even sure that the actual experience is important, but only the way that we perceive and react to it.

Further evidence of my parent's dislike for each other became evident when Dad was about eighty-five and could no longer find his way to work or back home. He became confined to the house most of the time, sitting in a recliner, while mother sat across from him in her recliner. He would get somewhat agitated at times and repeat questions over and over. She kept him on meprobamate, a tranquilizer, to keep him quiet while she harangued him from dawn till dusk. When he died, and she was alone, there was no longer anyone at hand to control. My sister in law was the most active caretaker of Mom and Dad, challenging as it was. But over time, Mom became unable to take care of herself, retreating into a more tolerable world as a means of escape.

I was so angered by the knowledge of what went on in my childhood, about the behind-the-back stories, the way people treated me or the way I felt they treated me, that I finally let it explode on mother in the form of a letter. This was following dad's death of course. Unfortunately, mother opened the letter detailing her "lying" to me as a child and not sharing the reason for the intense undercurrents through which I was raised, read it to my brother and his wife, thinking it was a letter from her most obedient son.

She never got over my writing that letter and, with the absence of my Dad in her life, went downhill over the next two years. She finally died, the last two weeks of her life being under my care of course, as Fate would have it. About two weeks before her death, she had some sort of cardiopulmonary episode that sent her to the Clinton, Oklahoma hospital. The Internal Medical doctor taking care of her inserted an endotracheal tube and used heavy medication to keep her from trying to pull the tubes out. This continued for some time and my brother had her transferred to the Midwest City hospital where I was working as Chief Radiologist. I tried vainly to get the attending physician to remove her endotracheal tube so that she could communicate, for I sensed that was her fervent desire, even though she seemed in deep sleep. Her spirit was not sleeping, and that was what was calling to me. We even contacted the newly formed Ethics Committee of the hospital to meet. It included a representative of the Administration, the hospital lawyer, the attending physician, a local minister, myself and several others. I could not believe they would let her lie there, dying, without an opportunity to communicate. But the attending physician's fear of a lawsuit, in my opinion, negated that attempt.

So, I was left with the only option of visiting when I could since she was in the same hospital where I worked. I kept trying to talk to her and sense what she might be saying. All the old guilt feelings returned, since this was still 1988, before the Big Bang. I would stand there, beside the bed, holding her hand, asking for forgiveness through my anger at her leaving me like this. The last time I saw her, her only communication was one dried and lonely tear that extended about three quarters of an inch down her left cheek. It had so much meaning in it that I had to write the following poem.

85

THE TEAR

A life of pain for worldly gain
Is what I finally saw in her
She never knew twas all in vain
But she is all I had, Dear Sir

I struggled too, for many years
Confused but confident was I
To gain her love but shed more tears
Before the two of us must die

The schism came before the bar
And some enlightenment did obtain
But the hurt had gone too far
And time was short for much to gain

But when the final crossing came
Twas not too late for recompense
When life had passed from her old frame
A final gesture made wholesome sense

A tear beneath her left eye to say
"I'm sorry son, forgive me dear."
My beloved Mother on Heaven's way
All is forgiven, now all is clear.

A few months before this, my thoughts were not as gentle as I was still in full revolt from processing the information of my childhood of touch deprivation. A child knows when it is being touched out of love or out of guilt. I was in the throes of crumbling, but when the lowest point is reached that is when one can build the best as the chaff is blown away.

WHEN DOES ONE DIE?

She died to me when I was born
And expelled from uterus torn
Just in the way and not desired
Better had this one not been sired.

There is a void that was never filled
A work of love that was never killed
But since it was not ever offered
It follows that it was not ever proffered

To build on something that was not there
A trait that should be nursed with care
This trait was never given a chance
Instead of love, was given a lance

Learn to love and to be loved
A thought into my mind is shoved
There is no basis to begin
There is no start, there is no end

What do I do to feel this joy?
That I never felt as a little boy
Simply in love to hold one near
My empty heart would greatly cheer

I'm struggling now to build a tower
For which I do not have the power
Tis hard to build a tinker toy part
Without the toys nor where to start

SPACE

The race goes cross the sky
In close pursuit am I, sometimes
Trying to grasp but losing hold
Words and signs too far apart
For me to gain foothold
And I fall through the cracks
I KNOW. I KNOW

This Gemini is truly twin
One repels the other
I am not even in the chase
They will each wear down the other
Then I will see

There are several ways one can think about life and the possibility of an afterlife. Mine seems to constantly change, as the "knowings" come. We either believe there is a spirit world or we don't. My good friend and neighbor in Creede, Colorado says "When you be dead, you be dead." That certainly is one way of looking at it but it does not satisfy my longing to want more out of my existence. Most of us have been taught that there is always a beginning and an ending to everything. I like to think that is not true about the existence of our souls, trying to get out of the traps of the human mind, set by centuries of closed-mindedness and the seeking of power over others. The possibility of "no time" becomes more and more palatable for me, the more I think about it and as my consciousness raises. Goodness. I do hope my consciousness is raising.

I am not telling you all this personal stuff because it is fun to do or to juice up the book so that people will buy it. I am telling it because it helps explain how I let circumstances of life decide who I was instead of deciding the circumstances that I could create. My folks sure had not done it so well and they both died very difficult deaths, not having a clue who they were, why they were here or where they were going. I finally decided that was not going to be my fortune, and I realized it did not have to be theirs.

We each can choose. We each have total control of our perceptions, how what we experience affects us. We do not have to hold onto emotions and let them destroy our lives. I have learned to have an emotion, experience how fantastic it is, and then let it go so that it does not become a controller of me. Yes, and that includes all emotions of depression, hate, love, etc. We can have emotions and understand they are fantastic, no matter what kind, and can only be experienced on this Earth. Don't ask me how I know that, but I do. It is what we are here for.

This was brought home to me so vividly in April of 2003 with the passing of my dear friend and drum teacher Babatunde Olatunji. He was seventy-five and in very poor health, having lost his vision, kidneys and in need of amputations secondary to diabetes. He is the first human with whom I have rejoiced at his passing, celebrating his life and not having to experience the much over rated grieving process.

11

MOMENTS OF HAPPINESS

You might legitimately ask if there were any good things about my childhood. It is so easy to remember what I consider bad experiences. Do you remember when I thought, at age fifteen, that I hoped that I didn't wake up at sixty and find out that I had done it all wrong? Well, that didn't happen. It was at age sixty two, and my thinking at that time was "My God! I have done it all wrong." But, that is just not true, as I would later understand. It was necessary to experience what I did experience so that I would be able to understand, to a greater degree, where others are in their journey. How many people do you know who have felt unloved or unlovely? I know that feeling.

One of the happy times in my childhood was in some of the ways we played, inventing new games, at least new to us. One of them required a tough Army blanket and two pairs of roller skates (with metal wheels no less). I never saw girls doing this as they limited their activities to less raucous games. With skates attached firmly to our feet, we would spread the blanket between us as we waited for the "sure to come" blast of wind to make the blanket billow like the sails of a pirate ship in the Caribbean. Our Caribbean happened to be a rough concrete street with mathematically placed chasms filled, or partially filled with black tar. Did you know that we chewed tar sometimes if no gum was had? When the mighty sea wind came, we were jerked forward, gaining frightening speed quickly, not realizing we could just let go of the blanket and set anchor. Surely, Guardian Angels were watching over us as we were propelled across the sometimes busy intersection onto the next leg of our journey. I wonder what the passing drivers thought, and said? Several pavement burns attested to our great adventure.

Some of the happiest times were in Colorado, vacationing. The only place that we seemed to be a normal family was in our cabin in Creede, Colorado. It was built on a hillside overlooking the small mining town, and we vacationed in it a couple of weeks each year. Six large pine trees hid it from the view of any gazing up from below. It was far enough above the town that one could sit in the outhouse South of the main house, leave the door open and contemplate the town, or one's navel, whatever turned them on.

Dad had bought the place in 1942 for $1,000 cash. That was a lot of money then. We were on gas and a bunch of other kinds of rationing because of World War II. Growing up in an environment of the Great Depression of 1929 and the World War had to have a great effect on who we thought we were, on our aspirations of life. The Colorado cabin was a great getaway and Dad would no longer be working night and day, unavailable to us. Of course, if we really wanted to spend time with him, we had to learn to fish. Mother finally realized this, and even though she did not like fishing, fell in with the group.

We got to hike many miles along beautiful streams, catching many fish and seeing much wild life. My brother once wandered off from the path, taking what he thought was a short cut, and got lost. About that time, he chanced upon a baby bear and knew that the momma bear would be close by. He ran as fast as he could away from that place, and must have been guided by his Guardian Angel, since he arrived at the creek where Dad and I were fishing.

The fun really started when we returned to the cabin with full creels and got to gut and clean the trout. We would have a race to see who could clean the fastest, a little game my Dad invented to get us to clean fish. I was very good at it. Then we would enjoy a meal of fried trout and potatoes, and play card games or dominos afterward. We would get so tickled and because of the constant laughing, it became difficult to breathe and I would have to lie on the bed to recover. Now, that was pure fun and all the hurts of the past were forgotten during those moments.

Dad loved the place so much that he may still be there in spirit. Once, about six months following his passing, we visited the old cabin. I was sleeping in a twin bed in the fairly large but sparsely furnished living room. I awakened about

6:00 AM to see Dad, wearing his fishing gear, walking across the room heading for the door. I was too surprised to try to say hello. A few days after that, as I was standing on the road in front of the house early in the morning, I looked to my left and about twenty feet away was dad, looking at the vista of the little town below. I did try to say hello, but got no response. Even so, I am convinced he had his moments of happiness like the rest of us, in that mountain cabin.

12

JOY OF THE DRUM

Now, somewhere in this book must be a recalling of the names of those who helped me find drumming, and to continue in it, since the drum has played such an important part of my life.

I believe I told you that Heather, at Esalen, gave me a one hour introduction to the African hand drum. That was an awesome experience and showed me how the drum can change one's direction in life. And that was only a one hour event! But that observation remains true to the present time, and most of my drum workshops are one to two hours long. It does not take "magic" long to work.

That first lesson was in November of 1991. Fortunately, Gordy Ryan, Master Drummer and a member of the group Drums Of Passion, was giving a workshop by the name of *Drumming & Massage*. I was to find that the energy and dynamic processes involved in both instances were similar.

The workshop was given in March of 1992, so I signed up, a little leery of the massage but also wanting to experience it. Peggy Horan, the chairman of the massage school taught the massage part. The class was mostly young people, which was a stress as I tried to keep up with their faster brains and reflexes.

We had three, two hour classes each day for a week. It was very difficult for me as I tried to master the hand techniques and remember the rhythms. By the end of the week it felt as if I would never learn to drum, but I was still convinced it had to be my voice for sharing joy. Dana, a blonde woman in her thirties was also in the class. She was almost as slow as I was, so we sort of paired off with the drumming and with the massage. That was a stress since I was the one with touch deprivation syndrome, practically no self esteem, and I was to share massage with a pretty blonde. My emotions raged, "Should this be a sexual experience? Should it not be a sexual experience? Was it wrong to do this?" So, I pretty much closed my mind and made it a non-sexual experience.

In my first Esalen experience I had heard and danced a bit to "Enigma," a fantastic bit of music, and very erotic sounding. I liked that. I bought a cassette during the drum workshop and played it once while Dana and I were alone practicing drumming. She stood mostly still while I cavorted like a bird doing a mating dance around her. The heart had the beat. The body did not.

The drum week ended and as I was sitting with Gordy, the drum teacher, and Peggy, the massage teacher, during coffee time, I arranged for Gordy to build a djembe (African drum) for me. It seemed rather expensive but justifiable. Peggy asked me what I did for a living and I told her I was a physician. She looked surprised and said, "I thought you were a clown in a circus." I suppose that was a slam, but it did not bother me. I must have acted the part in the early part of my re-creative experience. In fact, I try to act the clown when I do workshops, attempting to put the participants at ease.

Not long after that I met Rosario Corelli, a traveling drum teacher from South Carolina, who now lives in Taos, New Mexico. He helped me greatly with the drum basics and with the most popular African drum rhythms. I bought my first Ashiko drum (a cone shaped drum) from Rosario which had a goatskin head. For some reason, the head split not long after I got it. I had some cow rawhide, so thought I would try to replace the head myself. Working with the very thick skin was not as easy as I had thought it would be, even though it had soaked in water for twelve hours. I barely got it on using screwdrivers, pliers, clamps and a few well chosen words. The sound of the drum with the new cowhide head just blew me away. It was very deep and mellow, somewhat like a conga drum. It has remained my favorite drum and is well liked by women who seem to have an affinity for the lower sounds.

Then I had the urge to make a drum to see if I could create the chamber that produced the sound that had become so important to me. Somehow, (a synchronicity) I met a young man named Joel Tree. His last name was an adopted one since he actually lived in a tree, his iron bedstead lashed to the limbs. After being blown from the tree a couple of times by Oklahoma winds, he decided to park his bed on terra firma but finally decided it was easier to move to Florida. A small group of drummers would occasionally drum under his tree by the light of a small campfire. Joel worked for a Medieval Show and kept their equipment in good condition. He also was an excellent drum maker and showed me the process. My first attempt at drum making was very messy, frequently with more glue winding up on me than on the drum. It took three weeks to finish the first drum, after two grotesque failed shells had to be destroyed because the twenty wooden staves went every which way. Finally, it was done and I was as pleased as punch to find that it had a marvelous sound, much like a larger drum. It was my first "child" and I still have it.

While not much of a drummer, I was like a child playing anywhere and everywhere – by the side of the road, along the main street in Creede, Colorado, just about any place that would not cast me out. I started very early in my learning process to share what I had just learned with others, not worrying about what they would think about my attempts at drumming. In jest, it is somewhat akin to what they say about surgeons, "Learn one, do one, teach one."

Once, while visiting in Las Cruces, New Mexico, I stopped at a New Age store, took my drum inside and asked the lady proprietor if I could play it. I don't know why I did that, but I did. As I became lost in what I was doing, that my harmonica playing son would say is being "in the zone" a young lady came in and listened to me for a while and asked how long I had been playing. When I told her, she responded that one can't play like that in four years (I think that was a compliment). She explained that I must have been a drummer in a past life. Since I don't like to argue, I accepted her reasoning.

I encountered Babatunde Olatunji at a weekend drum workshop that he gave in Taos, New Mexico. I had taken two new drummer friends with me from Oklahoma by the names of Rob and Shaun, both fantastic drummers. I learned much about drummers and drumming from them. I approached Baba with some difficulty since everyone there wanted to touch him, and if possible, speak with him. After all, he was very well known in the drumming world and had taught such awesome drummers as Gordy Ryan and Mickey Hart (formerly with the Grateful Dead group). I put my hand on his shoulder and felt the energy that he radiated. He turned to me and I said, "Baba. I am Jim Arnold, a friend of Gordy Ryan's." He said, "Oh. Are you the one who is an MD?" Another "just blew me away moment." But that is what Baba does, spreading his beautiful spirit energy so naturally. There must have been over one hundred drummers there and when Baba sang, you could hear his voice over all the drums.

I then took a week long drum workshop from Baba at the Esalen Institute on Big Sur in Northern California. What an honor that was and my first teacher, Gordy Ryan, was there as well, playing the djun djun for Baba. Could it get any better than this? I was learning to relax while I played, not being as self conscious as usual. Sometimes, when drumming with Gordy at his workshops, I would almost be unable to play, being so tense from wanting him to approve of my playing. Baba has a way of saying "Be where I am." And if one was, then the drumming came easily and quickly. I use his technique when I teach my own workshops.

13

THE DRUMS SPEAK

LIONS AND TIGERS

Who hasn't been thrilled by the primordial sounds of the Lion and Tiger as they growl their feelings throughout the jungle? Is it surprising then when the human soul is awakened by the sound of the African hand drum? What does it touch within each of us, the low sound of the vibration of the animal drum head resounding through the tree that makes the shell of the drum?

Is there magic as the energy of Mother Earth is allowed to proceed through the feet, legs, heart and arms of the drummer, as the rumblings are encouraged to pass back into the Universe? Perhaps the magic is in the appropriate expression of the innate worth and beauty of each of us, giving vent to that inner child in a total and non-competitive sharing of our own worth.

Children are natural drummers and dancers (dancing being a way of drumming with the feet and body) until we teach them not to do so. Much of life is lived suppressing who we are in an attempt to be what we feel others want us to be.

As a former licensed minister and self-destructive Medical Doctor workaholic, I was once one of those children until the age of sixty-two when I developed a degree, of sorts, of self esteem and began to self express. The African hand drum and Australian didgeridoo have become my way of sharing my joy of life, helping others to approve of themselves.

Many of us have never allowed ourselves to be children, trusting in our own worth and beauty, and have spent our lives seeking approval when we have never even approved of ourselves. Then how can we be who we are and seek to find peace of mind if we feel it has to come from outside of ourselves?

How can we be the creative beings that we are, seeking the best for ourselves and therefore for all those around us if we feel not worthy of learning and sharing what we do learn with others, helping them to extend themselves more than they can imagine?

The simple expression of self through African polyrhythms on the drum and gentle blowing of the breath of Life through the didgeridoo has a great deal to do with freeing ourselves of our own feelings of inadequacy.

Music has long been known for its ability to soothe the soul and can be just as effective in awakening it.

CONNIE'S STORY

One of my favorite stories, which I sometimes share during drum workshops, concerns a middle aged lady, whom we shall call Connie.

It was about three years ago, and I received a short email from her saying that she had heard of me and thought that she might like to try drumming. Saginaw, Michigan, her home, is a far piece from Oklahoma City so the little gray cells in my brain started to create some way for this lady to drum.

My heart had to get into the process and led me to the thought that I must get Connie a drum, but she said that she could not afford one at the time. Things had not gone well for her, and the church that she had attended for so long no longer wanted her. She was not happy with the position which she held at the time, the Director of a mausoleum. Red flags were going up here and there for her, proclaiming a time of change. I felt deeply honored that I might become part of that.

"Spirit" let me know that I was to give Connie a drum, and I have learned not to argue with that part of my Greater Self. Of course, it was only natural for her to say that she could not accept the gift I was offering. Having had my own problems in the past with being able to accept a gift, feeling I was not worthy of any gift, it was easy to understand her reasoning. But, also having come to the place where I approve of who I am and can graciously accept a gift, it was incumbent upon me to tell her that even though she did not think herself worthy of any good thing, I could see and know of her innate worth and beauty.

For her to accept the drum as a gift would be part of her journey of learning self love and acceptance. I believe she may have cried a bit as this was occurring, and she could not believe that someone loved her enough to give her a gift. The drum was shipped to her, and the next step was to find a way to help her learn some basic drumming techniques. She mentioned that if I had Yahoo Messenger, as she did, we could actually converse in real time. I could play the drum rhythms, as she would repeat them and then play them with me. When I could not hear her playing, I knew she was on the beat but when I could hear her, she was not.

You know, perhaps that is the way it is with all of us. When we are of one mind, we are not aware of any discord but only of "Oneness." On the contrary, when we are not of one mind, in love, then there is the noise of discord, of judgment, of competition.

Connie learned fast and soon was deep into finding and drumming the rhythms of her own heart and soul. Her voice changed as I recognized the sound of joy and peace and felt the excitement through which she was going. Shortly thereafter, she quit her job and opened a New Age store which has been expanding ever since. She started publishing a Newsletter and has a wonderful Internet Web Page. She is happily remarried and when we communicate via email, I know that her heart is full of love.

She once called me, by instant email and asked "Who are you? Are you an angel sent to help me?" I had to say yes because I feel we are all angels sent to help each other. We just do not remember it

THE GENTLE GIANT

One of the most meaningful drum workshops that I did, at least to me, was at a Living Center in Northwest

Oklahoma City. They called it a living center, but upon entering, little energy seemed to be present that would signify happy lives. I surveyed the elderly people sitting mostly in chairs around the periphery of the large room. The room must have once been a grade school cafeteria and the coldness of the red brick was almost overwhelming. Some of the overstuffed chairs toward the middle of the room were occupied by those who seemed more in charge of who they were.

I was introduced by the young manager of the clinic, even though no one seemed to be listening, and I had to wonder why he would be working in such a place. I thought that he must have great compassion and this was his way of expressing it. I am sure his salary was not what had enticed him there.

We managed to get about eight of the more robust residents formed in the best circle that we could. I had never been challenged like this and wondered what I was doing there. But, putting my faith in the ever magic drum, I did the best that I could and explained a bit about the meaning of the drums until I could see that my lecture was going nowhere, fast.

We did a few basic rhythms, although one could not really tell if the group had any rhyme or reason. But the few who drummed seemed to enjoy it. I knew this was not going to be a long session as I was not being buoyed up as usual by the energy of the participants. Those lined against the wall never appeared to move a muscle, many slumped forward with only their seat belt keeping them from the cold, concrete floor.

The most entertaining of the group was a tiny elderly lady, maybe not as old as I, who was trying to play my first-made drum, which was brightly colored and evidently piqued her interest. As we progressed, I noticed that she had quit drumming and had found two long cords hanging from the drum. She had grasped one in each hand and was moving about, to the rhythm, as if she were riding a horse. It did not hurt her feelings when we all laughed and she began to laugh with us.

The participant that blew me away was a young man, very large and about twenty seven years old. He had the mentality of a small child who could not talk. His energy alone as he found his own inner rhythms and played them on the drum, lifted me from my doldrums (Hmm. Nice word and appropriate in this story) and I knew it was good that I had come. He got my attention several times by making joyful noises and waving his arms and with a smile about as broad as his beautiful face.

As we finished, I asked the manager if I could give him the little drum that he was playing and was delighted when the answer was yes. He was so excited that he wanted me to give everybody a drum. Ah, the love of a little child.

I received a letter from his mother several weeks later telling me how much she appreciated the gift of the drum to her son and how he played it many times during the day, thinking that it would bring me back. I will not forget this gentle giant throwing me a kiss as I left the room.

Was the trip to the Living Center worth it? But of course.

RAFAEL DELPHIN, THE SHAMAN

I received a brochure from Paulo Mattioli, Master Drummer from California, about a drum workshop he was giving on the Hawaiian island of Maui in the year 2000. Although I do not like to travel long distances, especially by air since there are long walks to the next airplane in the large airports, it seemed "right" to go. I have learned to be open to my intuition, perhaps that female energy that had so long been ignored.

The rather long and circuitous drive from the Maui airport to the camp ground was tiring because of the very narrow roads, but it was also rewarding as the "jungle" was an awesome experience. The many small cascading streams, waterfalls and "Ester Williams" pools were a delight.

The first day of drumming with Paulo was extremely energetic, evidence of his great energy and drumming ability. For some reason, although I could keep up, it did not seem right. So, why had I come this great distance from Oklahoma? Just to see Maui?

Rafael Delfin, a young Mexican Shaman, seemed to be the answer to this question. He was there giving a workshop in the making of didgeridoos from the local bamboo and learning to play them. During this time, he would take each class member aside and do a blessing or didgeridoo session on them. He seemed to be unable to find a time to do mine. I must say that he is a very beautiful man, if men can be beautiful, and looking into his eyes was like gazing into the depths of the Universe. The day before I was to leave the camp, Rafael told me that we should go to a very beautiful pool, secluded next to the highway for the blessing. It was most beautiful as if from a jungle motion picture and he proceeded to swim, stand in the waterfall and do awesome primordial singing. Upon returning to land, he started to do my blessing with the didgeridoo, which is preceded by a chant. Before that could happen, and I again was sure my mind was going, I told him that his Great Grandfather needed to give Rafael a blessing, through me. I was going to be a "channel" which had never happened before, or since, and I wonder if it happened then.

Before the channeling, it seemed right to take my hair from the pony tail that I wear and "fluff" the scant remaining hair. Rafael looked at me and said, "I recognize you Great Grandfather." Just blew me away in one sense, but seemed right in another sense. I put my hand on his head, said what was to be said and finished. Rafael then did a most awesome chant and didgeridoo blessing, following that by presenting me with his personal didgeridoo. Did I consider that an honor. Oh my yes!!!

While confirmation is not always needed, it is certainly welcomed and was given in a very impressive way. As we were finishing our "Power" session, two women whom we knew, were just starting down to where we sat at pool edge. I should tell you that it is rare to have a pool to oneself but the Fates evidently wanted us to have this one. Both ladies told us, even though they had not witnessed what had transpired at the pool, that they had felt this great energy coming from where we were. I like that.

PRACTICAL APPLICATIONS

It would make sense to have some practical applications of what I have been trying to say, perhaps an incidence in my life or a true story. The following is an attempt to do that as I share with you a letter I recently wrote to a person who wanted me to do a drum workshop for a group of very intense people. She wanted to know why I drummed, and what drumming was all about.

It hinges mostly on what I am about, why I do what I do to share my joy of life with those who are ready for it and open to all that the Universe has for them. I don't really teach drumming. I help people find out who they are which has nothing to do with what they do, what their talents or gifts might be and so on.

I have found that the drum and didgeridoo awaken that something within each of us which might be called the soul, causing it to begin to remember how innately worthy and beautiful it is, without exception. There must be a subtle and perhaps subconscious realization that there is a need for change. Those who think they have a need for something outside themselves to be complete, will not be open to this but will remain in the competitive and judgmental part of themselves. Only when they have reached the point where they are about to take that giant step into their true self will it accomplish what I am here to help them accomplish. Fear will keep many, if not most of them, from taking that step because they do not know what lies there, most thinking they will loose the Kracken* which they believe lies within, that will destroy them as well as others.

*The Kracken is a undersea monster in Greek mythology, under the control of Zeus, which the god Poisidon unleashed to destroy any city that had offended him.

I must have complete freedom to be who I am, at the moment, following what I feel is guidance from my greater self, whatever that is.

I feel deeply that what I do is done as a gift, in gratitude for what I have received freely from the Light.

If I do harm to someone or try to hurt them, then I am actually hurting myself. When I judge others, I am judging myself.

Of course, I do not have to be correct but that is what I believe today. Nothing is written in stone and I look forward to changes that come tomorrow, whatever they are. I like the surprise of not knowing what they will be.

I will segue this into a recent happening. In May of 2003, I was asked to do a drum workshop for the Lakota-Sioux Tribe meeting in Colorado Springs, called the Star Knowledge Conference. I had done one for the same group in November of 2002 and thought it went well, but was pleasantly surprised when I was asked for a repeat. While I try not to rely on affirmations from others, it is certainly a desirable thing and I am able to be open to those instances.

It is so nice to discover that Native Americans can be open to African drumming and I had wondered if any would show up for my workshop, even though it was free and I furnished the drums. The scheduled time was 2:00 PM but the place was in some doubt since the rain prevented us from carrying out our original plans of drumming outside. The alternate site was a room just off the main dining room of the hotel, divided from it by only a partial wall. I sat there, surrounded by my children (drums) who were anxiously awaiting the arrival of those for whom they would provide so much joy. No one was there at 2:00, except me of course, so I just started doing some light drumming and meditation. A gentleman showed up at 2:15 and was surprised no one else was there. He scurried off and within 10 minutes, the room was full of drummers of all ages, including some young Braves and Grandmother Chandra, a holy person of the tribe.

I did my usual thing and got them started drumming and intended to bring it to a usual end in about an hour and a half. When I did the count down from one to four, which should have ended when we finished playing the fourth musical phrase, no one stopped. They just kept drumming. I was so amused and surprised that I had to laugh. Something told me to say that I was through and then to leave the room and go out of sight of the group. I did that and it made not a smidgen of difference as the group continued on without me. Even my reaction to this was a surprise and I started laughing, realizing that this was the ultimate compliment for a teacher, for the group no longer needed the teacher but proceeded independently.

I rejoined the group and we drummed for two more hours. By that time, hands were becoming bruised even though the drummers did not feel the pain. The distraction of free self expression and the effects of the endorphins put out by the body during exercise cause some degree of anesthesia. Still, it had to stop, so I entered the center of the circle, drum held by a sash over my shoulder and once again began a very slow countdown to a finish, hopefully. My voice, in a high pitch, rang out Onnnnnnnne, as I circled one hand in a wide arch over my head. The Twooooooo was done even slower, in a slightly lower voice as I crouched just a bit. A lower toned Threeeeeeeee came next as my body crouched even lower toward the floor. The hopefully final Fourrrrrrr came in the lowest voice I could muster, being almost on the floor and I actually did fall flat on the floor as I finished the count, as if I had passed out.

Did they stop? Yes, thank goodness, they all stopped at the same time. There was an eerie silence for a few seconds and then screams of joy and laughter as the group applauded themselves for such a fine job. Grandmother Chandra, who cannot speak but can scream, was screaming her ecstasy as she wanted to continue drumming.

The group quickly broke up but a young Indian male, about 40 years of age, very tall and thin, stayed and looked at me. Under his arm was the little black djembe (African drum) that he had been using. He asked if he could buy it because it seemed so special to him. I had already noticed that this drum was the one that had come to me with a large crack in one side and I had to use a rasp to level the pieces after I glued them together. It left a large "scar" of deep brown color against the painted blackness of the rest of the drum body. As I looked into his eyes, it was obvious to me that he had his own "life scarring" with which he was dealing and had identified with the drum.

His eyes seemed troubled to me and I told him my impressions of the moment and how it related to him. He nodded and affirmed what I sensed, knowing its truth. He asked how much would it cost. My first reaction was to say, knowing it had cost me $180, even with the cracked side, "Would you be able to pay me $150 for it?" Before he answered, my question leaving a feeling of incompleteness within, I then offered it to him for $100. That caused no relief of whatever it was I was feeling and it became clear to me that I must give the drum to him as a gift. As I began to understand the dynamics of the situation I was filled with a most wonderful energy that cannot be described by words. So, I told him that he must accept the drum as a gift, because I was giving him part of me, recognizing that we were one. If we were one, then I was giving the drum or gift, or love, to myself as well as to him and that is when it actually became mine.

I have never had a feeling like that and it brought me to joyful tears as he actually understood what I was saying. His eyes were now those of love, and not of fear and my gift returned to me a thousand fold. His closing statement as we parted was "You are one in a million." How sad if true, that such wonderful expressions are so rare and how true that what just happened there was what we should all be about.

TRIANGLE: A NEW LIFE FORM

Following my "successful" psychotherapy experience with Dr. Francis Smith-Jones, and a session with the astrologer Gloria Star, I had what may be called a day dream or a day vision about the three of us. We were standing in a triangle configuration on a mountain top, holding hands. We started revolving, which rapidly increased and we soon became just a blur. We burst into a blinding white light which rocketed into space as would a comet, becoming a new life form.It was a reminder to me to not see myself, or others, within the framework of limited labels.

HOW I MET WILEY HARWELL

It will be obvious to many how thoughts, ideas, excitement, knowledge, and energy are passed from one person to another and how that progresses exponentially. It is no different with the sharing of what I call spirit energy by using the African drum and Australian didgeridoo.

Drumming, like laughter as you know, is infectious by just being around those who are laughing. Sooner or later, you just have to join in. The healing effects of laughter are well known. Those of hand drumming are known by some. The temptation to drum with music or even the constant and regular sound of the clicking of the car's windshield washer is evidence of this. How many of us just cannot refrain from keeping the beat to the car's radio while we tap on the steering wheel. We have all seen many individuals waving wildly and singing, to the rhythm from the car radio.

As I mentioned earlier, the first sound that I heard during my own re-birth was the African hand drum. Its sounds have not been lost since that first hearing, as I share my joy of life through this instrument. I began very early in my drumming days to facilitate drum workshops but which professional drummers might call something else, since I cannot read music. It seemed a way to touch the soul part of us, the beautiful part of us created in love. I cannot teach good drummers anything about drumming, but I can help beginners connect the sound with their own inner beauty and worth.

Having read *Celestine Prophecy,* and realizing and feeling the wonder of its message, I signed up to take a class about the book at a local church. Arriving a bit early, and usually carrying a few drums "just in case," I started playing one while sitting in the old suburban. A young man passed as I was playing, and I did not stop as I would have in the past because of a fear of someone "hearing" me. I wanted him to hear me and be curious, and I didn't even know who he was. He entered the church but came out immediately and walked to where I was. His question was, "What are you doing?" As we talked, I learned he was the lecturer for the class that I came to attend. We talked about it for awhile and during his lecture, he told the group that he felt it to be very important that they be allowed to drum. The young man's name was Wiley Harwell, a psychotherapist with a local practice.

This led to a fairly regular drumming at Wiley's psychotherapy office in Norman and his continued use of the drum for his friends, clients and family.

ESALEN REVISITED

I like to remember those high and exciting "energy moments" of my journey to freedom. One of those was my third journey to the Esalen Institute. During my first trip to Esalen, I had surfed the Internet, trying to "feel" an energy person with whom I could make contact within the Carmel area. On the list of those on AOL in that area was a Rick Phillips who lived in Carmel Highlands. It seemed the right thing to do to email him. He was in his eighties and referred me to his wife, Janice. She graciously invited me to lunch with them on the palisades overlooking the Pacific Ocean.

To take the course in drumming at Esalen, I had to either take or send a drum ahead, and asked Janice if she would accept it for me and I would pick it up later. She agreed, so I sent the drum and another that I had made for her at the same time. After arriving in their Spanish style home, I gave her a short lesson on the drum, but Rick only observed us for a short time because he was the cook for the dinner.

After leaving Rick's home, I went to the local outdoor market and noticed an elderly lady trying to make a decision over which artichokes to buy. I had just learned about artichokes from Janice and felt that I should speak to this woman. I was learning to be open to the guidance of "spirit" and was never surprised at the outcome. Keep in mind that this is an area of millions of people, visitors and locals in a very popular resort in California. I picked this one woman with whom to connect. My opening remark was "Pardon me, but my good friend Janice Phillips just taught me about artichokes." She turned to face me and excitedly said, "Janice is my best friend." I had no more doubts about life's synchronicities, those happenings that most call coincidences.

About a month following my visit to Janice's home, the telephone rang and the excited voice of Janice was on the other end. "Jim," she said. "You won't believe this. We are having the annual Carmel run for cancer (which goes by Highway 101 next to their home) and Rick is sitting on a chair by the highway drumming on your African drum." Ah yes, the drum IS magic.

"WIND GULL"

Approximately two years after my BIG BANG in November of 1991, I received a telephone call at my home in Oklahoma. A gentleman asked me if I did African drumming, and the "yes" answer elicited a request to visit me. When he arrived, he told me this story as reason for the telephone call. He lived in lower California and had a computer company which sold their wares to Tinker Air Force Base in Oklahoma City, not far from my home. He frequently would fly to Oklahoma, rent a car and drive to Tinker to do training for his computer programs. This time, as he was driving on the interstate highway in Midwest City, "something" told him to turn off and kept directing him to a drum store called Just Drums. Upon entering the store, he asked the clerk if anyone close by played African drums. They knew me, gave him my name and he made the call.

We talked for a while, drummed a bit, and I told him the story of my re-creation or re-birth experience which involved sea gulls, much like the book *Jonathan Livingston Seagull*, although I had never read the book. He was touched by the story and asked if we had a guitar. I got my wife's guitar, which he tuned, and then played and sang a song he had written previously and which had lain dormant 25 years. It was called *Wind Gull,* and was the story of my re-birth. This was the first time he had performed it. After we cried a few tears of joy, he gave the song to me.

JOEL TREE AND DOGS

It became obvious after I started drumming that it had an effect on animals, particularly dogs. In the early years of drumming with others, it was my good fortune to meet a young man who called himself Joel Tree. A group of us, about five people, would drum under his tree at night, in the light of a large bonfire. One particular night, we started drumming a most fantastic rhythm which none of us had heard before. When we stopped, I told Joel, "That was a great rhythm that you came up with Joel." He said it was not from him. He thought it was from Jack, another drummer. And Jack said "No. It was from the tree." Now, who was going to argue with that?

The first time I drummed with Joel, on my first visit to the farm, was in the daytime. We were sitting on the wooden porch, drumming. As I played, a huge dog, actually half dog and half wolf, came up to me and looked at me for an instant. I knew it was too late to run, so I continued drumming. Soon, he came closer, sat down next to me, and leaned against me the entire time we played the drums.

It is well known that music affects humans and animals, but there are specific instances worth mentioning. One such incident occurred when my wife and I were visiting Creede, Colorado during the summer. I had also learned to play the Australian didgeridoo and had brought some with me. A friend of ours, part Native American, decided to celebrate Summer Solstice at her house next to the Rio Grande River, as the beautiful mountains looked on. Grace asked me to use the didgeridoo to honor the Four Directions. It was approaching Twilight and as I played the didgeridoo, several coyotes joined in, which amazed us all.

THE STAR KNOWLEDGE GATHERING

As spoken of previously when telling of my second drum workshop at a Star Knowledge Conference, my first such experience occurred in November of 2002. I was asked by Chief Standing Elk of the Lakota Sioux to do a drum workshop at the Native American Star Knowledge Gathering in Colorado Springs, Colorado. I had met Elk five years previously when I attended one of the Gatherings as an observer, but did not know he knew that I did African hand drumming. I asked him if he was sure and he indicated in no uncertain terms that he was. It was very difficult to believe that he would really want me to do this.

Within an hour of accepting the invitation, I turned my upper trunk a slight bit to pick up the cat from the back of a chair and POW, my back went out. The symptoms were exactly like those I had several years previously while developing a herniated lumbar disk. The pain shot down my left leg and my knee became numb. It was immediately obvious what was going on. This was simply a symptom of the negative feelings of doubt within me about doing the workshop, a remnant of poor self esteem. Evidently, there is cell memory of all things to one degree or another.

I decided that the ruptured disk would not keep me from drumming at the Gathering, so I started doing what I usually do for self healing, reciting one of my mantras and then going to a local massage therapist. Actually it was a man and wife chiropractic team who had recently moved to Creede. They did very little manipulation, but a great deal of energy work. It confirmed what I thought was deep seated insecurity.

Within a month, I was without symptoms and did not have to have surgery as on a previous occasion. This helped fortify my belief that symptoms are but an indicator of mind, body, spirit disharmony.

The trip to Colorado Springs was difficult because I had trouble with my eyes being extremely dry but my Spirit Guides got me to the Red Lion Inn, site of the Gathering. The energy was high as I met those with whom I would spend the next few days, not knowing what to expect but being open to all that the Universe had for me. The first thing that I did, after checking in, was to go to the enclosed courtyard, sit in the sun and play the didgeridoo. I knew it was going to be a good meeting when I saw two fat squirrels playing under the trees and "asked them" to come over to where I sat. They did and "asked" me if I had any nuts or other food for them. I told them to wait while I went to my room and got some cookies. They did and then ate the cookies off the top of my shoe as I enjoyed their love energy.

I had wondered why Elk wanted my energy at the Gathering and was soon to find out. My first group consisted of about 30 people. The slightly over one hour session was more than I could have hoped for. The group, who had never drummed before, followed my instructions as I asked them to do what Babatunde Olatunji would ask his students to do, "Be where I am." The sympathetic vibrations of all the drums caused my own drum to join in with the drumming energy.

The second day, about 10 of the original group drummed and two of the women, in their forties, became highly energized, shouting and laughing at what they were undergoing, gaining insight into their own worth and beauty. They both told me they had never had an experience like that. A more conservative man stated that the drumming had opened up something in him that he had never felt before and thanked me for it.

I usually do my work without charge even when I furnish the drums, as in this case. The overseer of the meeting, well meaning, came in as the group finished drumming and asked them to give me a love offering. I really do not like to do that and the reason became obvious. A couple of people put twenty dollar bills in the basket as the others looked on. Many did not have that much money to give and several had none so they felt guilty in not being able to give me something. One elderly man said he would try to bring some money the next day and a young man gave me a CD he had brought since he had no money. It turned into a guilt session, like those I had experienced many times in church. I learned very early in my fledgling ministerial career that one could make more money by accepting a love offering than by asking for a certain amount of money to conduct a service. Is it possible that those giving the offering might possibly by trying to buy something? Hmmmm.

It took away the joy I have in giving the gift. A gift is not a gift if it is paid for but then just becomes a bartering process. How difficult it is for humans to receive a love gift.

As I listened to a couple of speakers, it became obvious that some negative judgmental energy was present and my non-judgmental non-competitive energy was needed. This was not a judgment on my part, but an observation, as I have learned to observe the journeys of others.

There were several vendors at the Gathering with jewelry, trinkets, health remedies as well as psychics and mediums. One interesting Medium was Soltara, a pretty blonde lady who advertises that she channels Elvis. I enjoy learning what I can from many sources so I decided to have a reading by her. It was very noisy in the area where she had been placed so it took a great deal of concentration of both of us. She channeled several spirit entities for me and I was a bit surprised when she described one whom she did not know. When she described him, it sounded exactly like my deceased father, wearing his fishing garb. I passed that off as a coincidence.

Next came a tall man in a dark suit, wearing a top hat and carrying a song book. Soltara finally recognized him as Abraham Lincoln who was contacting her because of a project she was planning concerning music. I was not ready for the next spirit to be channeled whom she said was St. Germaine and had a message for me concerning my past experiment with an energy producing machine. As far as I knew, that had not happened and in my mind I was saying "Boy. This lady is really confused." As soon as that thought was finished, she said "Do you remember when you were on the beach in Florida and saw the UFO outlined in a bright light and you saw the pilot and were one with him? Then because of the fear of being taken off with him, you dropped back into your body?" I doubt that there have been many times in my life when my jaw dropped in amazement as it did then.

It was a true happening with minimal variations. I had been at Flight Surgeons school in Pensacola and had been at one of the nearby beaches on a sunny day. What I thought I saw was a low flying Navy airplane like I had been flying in pass by in front of me, flying very low. I did not see it as a UFO but didn't believe in them at that time. I did see the pilot clearly, outlined brightly in the sun. I felt as if I were one with him and knew his family and some details about his life. Suddenly, I felt I would be taken off with him if I did not return to my body. Needless to say, I told no one about this because I did not want to appear crazy. Am I a believer in channeling of spirits? I think so.

The final big blast came to me in the way of a reading by one of the Mediums in attendance, Kari Chapman. I have never experienced such an event as several spirit entities were channeled for me and who provided information about why I am here and confirmed who I am. It was one of the most powerful thirty minutes of my life.

The journey back to Oklahoma started at about 4:00 AM, since I was unable to sleep after all the excitement of the past two days. As I drove South on the Interstate Highway, the sun was trying to rise and its flames were licking the underside of the clouds in the East. What a great show the Sun was putting on for me. In the southeast sky was a ten mile dolphin-shaped cloud draped over a very bright blue patch of the Universe that surely must have been a portal to another dimension. Just to the North of that was a most unusual and huge cloud, shaped like a ring and standing out from the rest being definitely different and like nothing I had ever seen. It immediately reminded me of the Eye Of Horus from Egyptian mythology. The culmination of this show of the Universe, which I felt deeply honored to experience, was when a giant shadow came over the car. I gazed upward to see hundreds, if not thousands of geese making a left turn to fly directly over the car. I gave thanks to the Universe for this and continued, somewhat dazed, homeward.

116

14

WHAT I BELIEVE

Somewhere in this book, it would only make sense to tell in one chapter what I believe. I would like to think that the book in its entirety would relate what coming full circle means, and that would not need further explanation. I would also like to think that the book could be called a modern Paradise Lost-Paradise Regained, after Milton.

I have tended to shy away from this chapter because I do not want the reader to think that I am espousing any particular belief or way of life except that which he or she finds in their own heart. I am talking about freedom of choice here, freedom to decide who you are and how you want to live your life. I can only tell you how I try to do it, because I cannot have the journey or describe the journey of someone else. If you take away anything from this book, I hope it would be the right to love your self and to know that self is innately worthy and beautiful. If you do not start here, then the possibility of really loving others is much more remote, if not impossible, as is your ability to receive love.

At the moment, since I retain the right to change my mind at any time, I have a few basic beliefs, call them "truths" if you wish. I do not feel compelled to be correct so am not trying to convince you of anything. I do not have a belief system, for to me, that connotes something that MUST be followed which would negate being who you have come to be. You might ask, "What do you mean, who you have come to be?" I used to think that every thing was decided for us, by God or something "out there" and that I had no choice in the matter. I did not want to believe that, but I did for 62 years, never quite sure when I was pleasing or displeasing that controlling force, always watching me to see if I were good or bad. Not a good plan for peace of mind.

Having a belief system meant that I was always under the control of whomever decided what that system was, and I was comfortable with letting others decide that for me, like ministers, administrators, teachers, parents, the Pope and anyone else who KNEW all there was to know. Now, I do the deciding, and don't have to have physical proof to make those decisions. What I believe now comes to me as "knowings." I don't know any better way to say it, nor can I tell you how to get it or put into words what it is. It is almost like feeling the wind and knowing that something is there, even though I can't see it. My knowing is like my heart "feeling" spirit energy, if that makes any sense. It doesn't make much sense to me either, since human words are insufficient to explain spirit.

In a nutshell, and I have been considered that by many, I have a Knowing that before I came to Earth as a human, my spirit existed in the spiritual domain of the Universe, very likely in a spirit group where each spirit could have many Earth lives, with differing relationships with each other. Was there a beginning of this spirit, or an end to it? No (he says emphatically as if he knows everything). It has always been and will always be. It is difficult to ignore old beliefs such as there MUST be a beginning and end of everything. If I stuck to that old belief, I would be greatly limited in what I can think about existence. I sometimes, in my mind's eye, will transport myself to a distant star and sit there and observe what I can see of the Universe and my "lifeline" as related to it. It comes into view somewhere on the left and passes out of view somewhere on the right. Right in the middle is a tiny blip, which represents my Earth journey. It is so tiny that it can barely be seen but still remains important in my total existence, as I evolve spiritually. Oh Oh! New term. What does he mean by that?

I used to think as I read the book of Genesis, that "God made all that is," and it seemed to make sense. Over the years, trying to separate God from all that is became more and more of a problem. In the last few years, I read that verse as saying "God BECAME all that is." Now, that made much more sense to me and would explain when Jesus said, "You and I are One." and, "The Father and I are One." If you wonder why I quote Jesus, it is because I believe he is one of the Ascended Masters. That would take another book to explain. It actually makes me part of Creation, of the Creator, never having been separate from any thing that is. If I am part of the whole, then

118

what I experience has an effect on everything that is. Someone explained it this way to me. If I am a drop of water and the Ocean is the Universe, then I am a part of that Ocean, but not all of it, just a vital part. Without all the drops, there would be no Ocean. A sort of nice way to think about it, if one is not blocked emotionally from doing that. So, what happens to me has an effect on the rest of the drops, and what happens to the other drops has an effect on me.

I think one nice way to go into this a bit deeper, although we are quite deep as it is, is to consider the power of combined energy of a group of people, who are like-minded. Prayer groups are a good example of this, as are healing drum circles which focus their combined energy for the healing of a person or some situation. Most of you have been aware of this in some form and want to believe it. This was brought to me in real time when I attended a workshop at the Monroe Institute in Virginia. During one of the evening demonstrations, the leader made two dowsing rods from coat hangers. He showed us how to find the edge of the energy field around our bodies. The field of energy extended approximately twenty inches out, more or less, for all of the 22 people participating.

He then had two of the participants leave the room, out of earshot, and told us to focus our energy on one of the two that had left the room. When they were called back into the room, we again checked their energy field. The one on whom we had not focused had the same small field. The other's energy field had enlarged beyond twenty feet. The same experience has been noted in studies by the American Medical Profession with an increase in healing of a person prayed for by a group rather than by one individual. Another study was done showing group drumming to have anti-cancer effects by raising the strength of the body's immune system. Amazing!

Let's see. Weren't we sitting on a star looking at my lifeline? I think so. So, the little Earth blip that I see tells me that this is a moment of spiritual evolution and puts it into proper place in my total existence. It would be much more difficult now for me to think, "Hey. This Earth thing is all there is." Sort of helps me relax and not make so much of what goes on around me.

I used to think that we didn't have a chance in this world, if we were obligated to keep all the rules since there are so many, whatever the belief system in which you find yourself. It helps me to relate to all that is and know that everything that has consciousness is a part of God, of Creation, of Light or whatever name one wants to give all that is. I cannot know more than that, until I reach full consciousness. That means different things to different people. To me, it is like an extremely short experience I had while fishing in the Colorado mountains. The area was filled with willows, making it difficult to find a place to put a hook in the water and the banks were steep that led back to the road. As I struggled up the bank, trying not to slide and break my nice fly rod, I suddenly had the most glorious feeling I had ever had. I didn't know what it was, but knew it was awesome and I seemed to have a tunnel of understanding that went to the center of the Universe. There seemed to be nothing that I did not know in that nanosecond, as if God and I were connected some way. Then, it stopped and I was left wondering what had happened. But, I knew it had happened and there was much more to learn while I was on Earth. When all the questions are not questions to me anymore, then I will have reached full consciousness and know my connection to all that is. When you, the reader, and I both know what is in the mind of each other, there will be no more deceit, no secrets and we will have reached full consciousness. I like to think that the first secret was the beginning of deceit. I can't do any better than that because these are just words and that was an experience.

So, I came here, knowing why I came, and the purpose. But to have the evolutionary spiritual experience that I came for, I had to forget the why of it and start from scratch. That also meant that I had to forget how innately worthy and beautiful the spirit, my spirit is, leading to the loss of self esteem or self love. My purpose was to remember, to regain that knowing of self love as I lived my life. I have heard that the new children, such as the Psychic Children, do not forget these things in order to help the rest of us to remember. I like to think that.

It has also become obvious that what I write here, that you are reading, has to be from my context of life, all that has happened to me in this Earth existence and all the thoughts that I have had and the resulting impressions and perceptions. It is almost like a set of finger prints, much different than those of any other soul, which would make each of us unique, or to coin a phrase "soul specific." Therefore, when you read these lines, you are getting impressions from them in terms of your own context of life, to how each word, sentence or expressed thought may fit into that context. You certainly cannot read it from my context of life. So, you may understand or not understand at all what I am trying to express. There is an old saying (all sayings are old) "We hear what we want to hear."

Please do not let that be confusing because what I am saying is important only to stimulate or process what you are reading, and apply it to you. I would hope that you would not summarily dismiss all that I say or accept all that I say but only take that part which resonates well with you, or feel that it applies to you. After all, the purpose of this book is to help you find and accept who you are, not who I am. I know your innate worth and beauty but what is more important is for you to know.

I also know that I have the option, right, obligation, honor, and responsibility to have what ever perception I wish to have as to whatever happens to me physically or emotionally. I do not have to accept the "usual" way of responding or thinking about anything that happens to me. If I want to grieve when a friend passes, I can do that. If I want to honor that passing soul and be joyful with it as it re-enters the spirit world, I can also do that, as I did with my teacher Babatunde Olatunji. I know that he is more present with me now than he ever was while in body. I know that I can always be in contact with that soul whether it is in the body or out of the body. I can refuse to believe in the impossibility concept. I do not have to keep a list of "goods" and "bads" of life and try to gain or avoid them, never really knowing what the balance scales are saying. I can take what Pope Paul II said in the late 1990's as he expressed his belief that "hell" is not a reality, but a state of mind.

WHOA! Where did that last statement come from? Yes, I can believe whatever I want to believe. If I choose to believe in a final judgment to decide whether I spend eternity in heaven or hell, then I will base what I do in life on that fear, never knowing for sure which way I will go. If I choose to believe that there is no judgment, no heaven, or hell, then I am free to live my life as I came to live it and to evolve spiritually as I came to evolve. When life is lived in fear, there is no freedom of thought because all thought and action will be based on trying to avoid what is feared, even as we try to avoid the conscious awareness of that fear. We may not talk or have conscious thoughts about it, but we are always trying to avoid dying and the expected judgment, neither of which exists in reality. We don't die. We leave the human container in which our spirits have lodged for a time. We are not judged, except by ourselves.

It has become very clear to me that when somebody judges me or thinks I am a kook, that does not say anything about me but does says where the one doing the judging is. You might say, when we judge others, we are really judging ourselves. When we accept others, we are accepting ourselves. Substitute the word "love" for the word "accept" and you have a very basic belief of mine.

As Lynn Grabhorn states in her book *Excuse Me, Your Life is Waiting,* when one puts out positive energy, positive energy comes back. When one puts out negative energy, negative energy comes back. When you go into a room where there are people, you automatically "know" who is angry and will shy away from that person. You will "know" who is putting out love energy and will be drawn to them.

Finally, I agree with many of the new children who say we did not come to Earth to learn or do this and that, but we came to remember who we are, that we have no limitations except those that we place on ourselves. We came to experience all that there is here to experience and as we evolve spiritually, the entire Universe, ALL THAT IS, also evolves in a positive way in that search for Self, for Home.

Perhaps, not finally, when I have reached full consciousness, all the above will become null and void. That is called change. That is called evolution of the spirit. That is what we are doing even as we speak. We have, together, EXPERIENCED evolution because we have made changes in who we think we are, as I write and as you read.

You might, if you have read this far, wonder just what I do believe about this life. And I can only share how I feel at the moment, for who knows what the next moment will bring.

This is what helps me to be who I am, to keep remembering day by day. As I thought, as a six year old boy when the heavens seemed to open to me as I stood in the yard by the house on North Grant Street, I AM part of God, along with all else that exists in the Universe. But, I let that knowing be taken from me until age 62. It returned in late 2002, while meditating at home.

The thought came: God did not create the Universe. God BECAME the Universe and all that is. So, that connects me with all that is and more closely applied, to all those sentient beings on Earth. The Oneness is so complete that whatever I do has some effect on the rest and what they do has an effect on me.

I like to think that while in the Spirit place, before coming to Earth and taking abode in a human body, I decided, along with my "spirit group," what I needed to accomplish while on Earth to foster my own spiritual evolution as well as that of those living here and possibly all beings outside of Earth. Since I knew the plan and how it would occur, it would be necessary for me to forget the plan upon taking on the human container.

I was aware of this plan for a very short time as a child but as the environment in which I lived began to influence me, that memory faded. Hence, it would be understandable that small children still have some contact with the spirit world and "see" and "hear" things that adults do not, much like a cat might.

Then, logically, it would seem that all others present on Earth are here for the same process, living out their lives trying to remember who they are and why they came. It seems that loss of self love, self esteem, is a necessary part of this, in most instances. This sets up a play of trying to get something we have lost, some calling that "salvation" or "seeking first the kingdom of God and all these things shall be added unto you."

It is not that others or situations are to blame for what transpired in my life; they were only opportunities or experiences for me to learn, to remember who I am, to regain self love. Without self love, I cannot really love another nor can I receive love because I do not think that I am worth loving. So, love of self must come first before the process of full remembering or full consciousness can occur.

My greatest epiphany came when I "owned" my own self worth and beauty and loveliness, at the age of 62. Then it was no longer necessary for me to seek approval because I approved of myself. I no longer judge myself nor feel compelled to judge others. It became possible for me to love others, not to judge them. It became possible to honor the journey of all on Earth, without exception, even though I might not agree with their way of life. Life became experiential and not competitive. I developed a desire to share my joy of life with those who were open to that sharing

Looking forward to the end of this Earth life became less frightening, knowing that I would be giving up this body and going on to another existence, perhaps in another life on Earth. But, it may also mean that this process might end when I complete the process for which I came and complete by fully evolving spiritually in this phase of my existence.

15

FURTHER REFLECTIONS

THE BLACKEST HOUR, STARLIGHT

I was recently reminded during a talk by the spiritual medium Mary Ann Morgan, author of *Living In The Moment,* that in order for some of us to wake up, we may have to be hit by a large two by four wielded by the Universe. So it was with me.

I was Vice Chairman of the Deacons at of a very large church in the Oklahoma City area, and that part of me which thought I should be a minister, a missionary, a workaholic and all the other things dependent on what "they" said I should be, was pleased. But, the main part of me, that part of my greater self, with which I had been created, was most unhappy with where I was. The battle between the different parts of me raged mightily in those days, and there were plenty of church leaders ready to enforce the guilt system in which I had allowed myself to be submerged. They had their own problems and were very quick to involve others in them.

One of the outstanding works of the church was a large outdoor meeting called Starlight (I don't think the stars intended to be blamed for this) which lasted a week. Guest speakers were invited, and emotions ran high as it seemed that all but a few would be convinced that they "had been found wanting." Pattie and I were sitting with the large choir as the guest evangelist told us "true" gory tales of the workings of satan. He invited any who wished to come to talk with the associate ministers waiting to help. I remember the blackness that descended on me and was totally confused since I thought that I had done those things I had been told to do all my life. I followed the rest of the choir leaving a scant few, including my wife who had not been convinced of her unworthiness. A large number of the audience was also filling to the front.

As I approached Brother Jake, an old truck driver turned minister; he looked at me in surprise and asked what I was doing. I could not answer other than, "I don't know." I cannot remember what was said after that, but I do know that I swam in the darkest parts of the Universe for the next week as I became bedfast. This led to my attempted suicide from which I turned away at the last moment KNOWING that this was not the way.

So, was this a bad experience? No. It was just an experience, but an important one which helped me open up to all that the Universe has for me, the most important of which was loving myself. Because of that, I am able to share my joy of life with others in the ways that I do, helping them to lose their fear of death and judgment, love themselves and be open to all that the Universe has for them.

THE MONROE INSTITUTE

My search for self acceptance, and a desire to go out of body and find what really is "out there," led me to the Monroe Institute in Virginia. The institute had been established by Robert Monroe in order to explore the spirit world of energy by consciously altering the mind.

After three trips to Virginia, I never had the typical experience of which Monroe spoke, but I did have a few exciting times. One of note was during an attempt to go out of body which would mean for me, lying in bed on my back, listening to the prepared cassette tapes, toning by humming in an attempt to get the body to vibrate and then having my energy self rise out of the body, float to the ceiling and turn over to look down at "myself" lying there in bed. Seems an easy task, no? Being a cynic does not help and trying to get out of the way, so to speak, and let it happen has been my great downfall or block to experiencing what I know can be experienced.

Discussing this problem with our leader, I was told just to "pretend" it was happening and see what happened. That was certainly a plan. My first attempt seemed to be going well even though I knew I was pretending. My spirit or energy part of me started rising from my body, went to the ceiling and

126

turned over to peer at what lay below. But, and a big but, was that I did not see myself. Instead, I saw a human-sized, very white and typical Extra Terrestrial with large, dark eyes and a small mouth. Pretend or not, that brought me back to Earth quickly and ended the session.

Mustering up a bit of courage, I made a second attempt and with the same results. One final attempt to try to see "Will the real Jim Arnold please stand up?" had no better results. It was impossible for me just to say "Okay" and move on into the Universe and see what was out there.

REGRET?

And what am I to think about those early years of my Earth journey? Should I have regret for wasting precious time (and what is time?) and not getting more quickly to where I think I am now? Should I be intolerant and judge those decisions of youth and early manhood as bad, poorly thought out, or just a tool of the dark side?

On the contrary, I give thanks to the Universe that I was allowed to make those precious decisions in my own time, and in my own way, as I struggled to remember who I am and why I am here. Many decisions did not bring what I intended at the time but instead brought personal suffering. Now I understand that these decisions and the resultant suffering provided lessons/opportunities for me to overcome so that I could evolve spiritually. However, at that time, I thought that the purpose was to be able to claim my rewards in the nebulous place called Heaven, If we are lucky and have done nothing to anger the vengeful God of our creation. Is that not what the Christian Bible teaches?

I would not change anything that fell into my life, even those things considered unpleasant by most human standards. There were reasons for the way I perceived pain, pleasure and all things that happen to mankind. After all, I do have total control of how I perceive anything that befalls me, or stated in a more appropriate way, anything for which I have set myself up.

While I do not totally understand it, I have a "knowing" that those processes through which I have allowed myself to go in this Earth life were meant to help me in my spiritual evolution. The energy expended in all those times of my past has been the energy which propels that evolution. Energy is neither bad nor good, until we decide it is. It is just energy and we are blessed with the freedom to use this awesome power to make those decisions that all have consequences, many which seem unpleasant.

I don't expect to understand fully my present Earth life until I have reached full consciousness. However, I am learning not to judge myself or others since that would mean that we lack something that is not available to us, that we are incomplete and separate from others as well as from the Creator. None of that is true. As many are telling us in books and courses, we have never been separate from ALL THAT IS nor from each other. What affects one, affects all.

BOOKS THAT HAVE HELPED ME

Perhaps the reader would benefit from knowing some of the books which helped me on my journey of awakening. One of the first books that I read as I was consciously starting on my journey of awakening in the mid 1980s was written by Gloria Steinem, *Revolution From Within*. Having restricted reading to only medical and Baptist accepted religious literature, it was quite a jump to read a book by this well known activist.

Unknowingly, I was responding to my own inner voice while watching Ms. Steinem on a TV interview. There was something in her voice, and a light in her eyes, that told me to read the book. It was written, in my opinion, on a higher level of communication than emotion alone and was therefore "Okay" for me to read. What cinched the truth of the content was when Gloria answered a complimentary letter that I had written to her. She simply stated her agreement with what I had said. Then, I knew there was something different for me in life.

The next book was *Dance While You Can* by Shirley MacLaine, a more emotional appeal for me and the next book to which I was guided, as I feel all the books were, for me to read. It seemed to help me come down off the intellectual high horse on which I had been sitting, the one saddled with fear to be whom I came to be in this Earth existence. As with Gloria, I had to write a thank you note and received a blessing of a hand written note from Shirley to honor my thanks.

A friend from Chicago, an email pal, sent me James Redfield's book, *Celestine Prophecy,* and started me on the journey of feeling and experimenting with my own energy field. Hearing James in person set the book in my mind and heart as the sharing of a very spiritual man.

Of course, the books by Neale Walsch will never be forgotten, especially the first volume of *Conversations With God* in which I learned it was okay to question anyone and anything, even God.

Many other books followed as I became open to their content. Several had to wait until I was ready for them and some had to be reread; all controlled by my Greater Self which I did not know existed at the time.

WHAT DO YOU WANT FOR CHRISTMAS?

As is my custom in early December of each year, I ask Pattie "What do you want for Christmas?" When instead of the "I don't know" or "It doesn't matter" or "Don't worry about it," I got the answer of "I just want peace and quiet." Before I could think, I asked "How would you like that wrapped?" Before she could think, she answered "In very quiet paper."

Isn't that beautiful, spoken from deep within each of us and a great message for both of us? After all, what else could we ask for that we do not have? We certainly have all those things physical that one would need, and more. But most are not satisfied with that. Would we be satisfied with peace and quiet? If it is real peace of the heart-mind, then I would have to say yes. That kind of peace would bring quiet even in the midst of great surrounding noise because it would mean we have found what we are looking for, self. When we find the love of self, there IS nothing else. All becomes love.

PEACE OF MIND

I think I must be in a controversial mode as I write these words today. What I seem to be seeing, in what a good friend of mine recently said, is that when everybody has all the money and material things that they think they need, then they can come to full consciousness. If that is what he means, then that is not where I am.

I feel that coming to full consciousness is a task of all Earth souls and that the struggle to get there, no matter what the environment of each, is the dynamo that runs the motor of spiritual evolution. I like the Bible's statement that one can find peace of mind whether they are prince or slave.

When in premed in college, I remember telling my wise old major professor, "Dr. Trent. If I can just make $1,000 a month, I will be happy." He said nothing but smiled. I now know why he was smiling. It is a common saying for people that being wealthy makes life easier and that is not a truth to me. Wealth, even having all that one thinks one needs is not what brings peace of mind. Nothing outside of self brings that. It does not matter what befalls our Earth body but it does matter how we perceive and react to it. It is totally, right now, within our control.

People are in the habit of getting themselves into places of great physical need, as well as emotional need, none of which is necessary for the existence of the spirit within the body and finding what we came to find, self. In fact, the more we have on a physical level, the more it can get in the way of seeing who we actually are and remembering why we came. To be able to love ourselves as we love others is not a function of wealth.

YOU GET WHAT YOU PAY FOR?

Wouldn't it be fascinating to discuss motivation, perception and the old concept, "You get what you pay for?"

That concept, to me, is invalid and is only a perception that we have taken as a whole so that we would not have to honor ourselves enough to receive a gift. We hasten to try to "match" any gift that is given to us, particularly on holidays, or else we feel guilty. But, I am not trained in debate and no longer seek to change anyone to my way of thinking as I did, in fear, when a young ministerial student. I could not tolerate someone disagreeing with me because then I would have to think I might be wrong.

To me, it is a matter of self worth, something we are usually told we do not have; religious writings especially tell us that we are "unworthy" of anything. Some accept that view totally, as I did once, and some do not. But it is the perception by which most live their lives.

Fortunately, I have nothing to prove so I don't have to argue with anyone about anything. I don't feel compelled to be correct, a human trait (or failing). I am not seeking approval because I approve of myself and I have to keep telling myself that when I am "slam dunked," by life. I do not set myself up to be hurt because what others do to hurt me only tells about them and not me. At least that is my thinking today. It may change tomorrow and that is okay. Today, I am here to share my joy of life in any way that I can with others, seeking to do no harm, trying to build up others in their own minds, and not tear them down to make myself look more than I am.

LOOKING FORWARD INSTEAD OF IN THE NOW

Some think WHEN we get this, then we WILL get that. This type of cause-effect thinking is no different to me than the religious view that "some day" we will get our reward in Heaven.

So, what we are saying is that we cannot have peace of mind or full consciousness now. We can only find it tomorrow, and not today. And tomorrow never comes with that line of thinking. If we require something outside of self for peace of mind, then we make this dependent on something that is constantly changing. Christianity is really a devotee of suffering today for a promised reward (maybe) in Heaven.

Instead of seeing all happenings as an experience from which we learn, we must classify or judge all things as "good" or "bad," forgetting that energy is just energy and is neither bad nor good. In our minds it becomes what we perceive it to be.

I maintain that the great Master teachers, especially Jesus, encouraged us to believe that we are already complete, already in a place, a state, where we can know that we are who we are and in that instance of acceptance, there is full consciousness or remembrance of who we are and why we came to Earth. Hmm, could that be what Jesus meant as "salvation?"

Even if, as some believe, we are really products of an experiment by ET's who originally created us, I do not believe that they also created the souls which occupy these containers. My thinking on that is subject to change.

As our earth scientists struggle with trying to understand the relationship of soul to human body, so I think that those ET's, if they exist, also struggle with that. Perhaps all sentient beings try to find God or Creator. I contend that it is not to be found in the intellect or in science, but in the soul itself, which cannot be dissected.

LOVE DOES NOT JUDGE OTHERS OR SELF

We have been raised to judge and criticize and to think that we are victims when we are only victims of our own perceptions of reality. This is the meaning of what Jesus said when he said that we should be "in" the world but not "of" the world.

It is a time of change, not of others "out there" but of ourselves when we accept the magnificence of who we are, which is LOVE. LOVE does not judge others or self. LOVE does not keep score or try to change others, but the extension of our love may be a changing force in the life of those around us.

Chief Standing Elk knew this very well when he called me to share my "energy of oneness" with the Native Americans at the Star Knowledge Conference. It is at a time when many tribes and groups want to be separate and be more exclusive than inclusive. This has been evident in religions as several large denominations begin to fragment into smaller groups with different beliefs. It should be a time of finding how we are alike instead of how we differ. I did not understand why he wanted me to do that until the second Conference when it became apparent.

I do not need to try to change anyone, only myself and the way I perceive who I am. As that progresses, the desire to try to change others passes and I can only love them. We cannot "argue" others to change. That only drives them farther into that which they already are. It is not an intellectual process. It is, as Chief Red Cloud says a "heart-mind" thing. And, I have no compulsion to appear "correct." I will not know, in the finality of all things, that which is true until I have reached full consciousness. Then, I will see myself as I am seen by "God."

A KNOWING

I can just "see" the spirit group of Jacob, John (names changed but real people) and his wife before coming to Earth to occupy the containers that they now have. It was a marvelous journey planned to bring out the most awesome emotions, feelings, and experiences that they could have. While they see it now as "bad," they originally saw that they result only in an increase in love of themselves and the Universe, as they evolve spiritually along with the rest of us. The physical construct is made by collective consciousness because of perceived needs and is not the reality that we shall soon know. All consciousness will profit from these many journeys and the awakening will continue.

There ARE so many things going on at many different levels of which we have no understanding but which will someday be revealed, even as the book The *Gathering*, speaks about. As I do not know the depth of understanding of my own

133

words, the author of that book may also not know, but we all can have a "knowing" within our heart-minds that all is going as it should. Only the moment is real-regret of the past and fear of the future holds no sway over us. It is all within our control. I feel about the Earth life as I do when I teach drumming and tell the participants that "You can't do it wrong!"

WHAT DO YOU WANT FROM ME?

Lately, when someone says they want to drum with me, I have taken to asking them "What do you want from me?" I think it is a fair question even though I realize that the person may actually not know themselves. I have written some poetry, some over ten years ago, and I am just finding out what I was trying to say.

One young psychologist had been to my house a couple of times and we drummed and talked. Well, mostly, I talked since I seem to like to do that. I finally asked him, George, what do you want from me? He thought for a moment and said, "I just want to hang out with you for a while." Well, that just blew me away because I couldn't understand why anyone would want to do that. Others have told me that they feel my nonjudgmental energy so they feel free to be who they really are, without secrets or deceit. I feel that when we have our first secret, that is the beginning of deceit. That may not be but it is how I feel at the moment.

The next time I hear from George, he has gone to the Esalen Institute on Big Sur and had had a life changing experience similar to mine. When I asked him what happened there, he said to go to the Esalen web page at a certain URL. I did, and there was a picture of his face with the caption "Afterglow." I did not have to ask what that meant. He is now in the practice of psychology in Oklahoma and intends to use the drum in his practice.

There is a minister in a nearby church who is sick of organized religion. He wants out but feels he cannot get out because of the medical insurance. When we were talking and drumming one day, I asked what he wanted from me. His answer was "I want you." I think that I know what he meant but fear keeps him from completing his search for what his heart really wants.

I am amazed, pleased and humbled when I hear these things but know that I am here for a purpose. Having been a Fundamentalist Baptist minister and a workaholic medical doctor has given me a certain credibility among some people who think that I know something that they want to know. I accept all, honor all journeys and try to be what I need to be to help each person find their own true love of self, even if they are not consciously aware of that.

Someone asked me once if I wanted to know when I would die. I answered no, but did not tell them why I said that. I feel that the future (although I do not believe in the Earth reality of linear time) is something that I want to be a surprise as I awaken each day to take on what is there as I evolve spiritually and have encounters with other souls.

I do not think that the future is written in stone but changes every time we have a change in thought or make a decision. I guess that would be called creative consciousness and if enough people think positive, loving things, then the future will change to match that thinking. I think that where we are now as an Earth society has been determined by that concept as well as the physical condition of Mother Earth with whom we are ONE.

It is so easy to get caught up in a belief system and then try to make ourselves and all around conform to that concept. It is time to rid ourselves of The Impossibility Concept and understand that we ARE the magnificence of God, Light, Creation, Creator or whatever one uses for that expression. I like to think that the statement Jesus made "Greater things will you do than I have done" is a true statement of the I AM-NESS of each one of us and of ALL THAT IS. There has never been a true separation from All THAT IS, only in our perception, and we have complete control of our perceptions and how we react to our environment.

135

SIMPLE

I wrote this note to a friend when she told me she did not like me calling myself "simple." In trying to enlighten her to my meaning, I wrote.

I say I represent "simplicity" because our existence and the owning of it is very simple. To me, it cannot be understood by words, yet the love energy behind the words is where truth lies. Sometimes I will write these things to you not fully knowing if they are worthy of remembering. Also, thinking about the last line in my book being something that will "grab" a person's knowingness, I came up with a thought, partially expressed but with not quite the "jazz" that I want.

It is not important what I wrote a minute ago, as you read it. It is not important what you will read next. It is of critical importance, in all dimensions that exist, that YOU know who YOU are at this instant and that YOU love who YOU are.

WHAT DO YOU THINK ABOUT RELIGIONS?

My life, at least until the age of 62, was mostly controlled by my chosen or "pushed upon" religion. Of course, it did not have to be that way. It was, as all decisions are, a choice that I made on my journey. I happened to pick the Southern Baptist Religion which was strong in my little home town and sort of vied with the local Church of Christ. If I had been in Afghanistan, I would have been Muslim, in Japan, probably Shinto, in China, a Buddhist, and so on. Or not. I would have had the ultimate choice in what I would take up as my guideline in the Earth life.

I wonder sometimes if I used the church as a surrogate family, not feeling comfortable in my own. There was certainly no lack of guidance there as the answer to all questions was a quoted scripture from those whom I considered infallible. I didn't realize these "authority figures" were on their own journey as was I, trying to ferret out the truth that they had been told was in the church.

So, I spent the main part of my life attending as many church services as I could, molding my life around religion and shutting out everything else that might have been helpful or at least a consideration for making wise decisions about life. In my married life, if I did not spend time in my workaholic profession, I spent the rest attending this or that at the church, dragging the family along with me.

I am not saying that your motivation for being a member of a religion is the same as mine was. Mine, in the truth of retrospection, was all about fear. Fear of death and fear of judgment following death. This is the mainstay of most, if not all religions. I could not see that until I lost the fear of death and realize the only judgment is my own. So, now I can live and share who I am in Love and really feel that God, Universe, Light, and other concepts are actually Love and that there is nothing BUT Love.

"Are you saying it is wrong for anyone to believe in a religion?" Of course not. I am not saying anyone is "wrong" about anything. What good would it be if all we came to Earth for is to follow a set plan without choices, all having one consequence or another? It would be boring and non-productive. Since I believe we have to forget why we came to Earth so that we could have the journey of spiritual evolution, there had to be total freedom of choice. I don't even believe in right or wrong choices but just that each choice has a particular consequence that leads us to the next choice. We can interpret that concept as good or bad but that puts us into a mix-master of judgment.

In other words, I do not regret ANY decision that I have made or ANY consequence of that decision. For me to be where I am now, in my awareness, it was necessary to have the experiences that I did. "To what purpose" you might say. One purpose would be writing this book. Another, finding my own lovely soul and being able to share that, shamelessly, with others through the "magic" of the African hand drum, the

Australian didgeridoo, healing energy, compassion and all those things that uplift others.

Perhaps the greatest purpose was to come to the point where I can look at others and see only Love. And, seeing that Love, I am seeing myself.

Experiencing the mishmash of life has been the dynamo that runs the engine of spiritual evolution to run headlong into the "place that we never left," HOME (Coming Full Circle).

A NEW PERSONALITY AND ATTITUDE

There are several occurrences following my "re-birth" that helped confirm the reality of that change, allowing me to discount the feeling that I had gone completely mad. One of the most notable was a malpractice court case in which I was involved which happened within two weeks following my return from the Esalen Institute.

The case had started three years previously and concerned a suit brought by a patient who had been treated in the hospital emergency room. I was the Radiologist on call at the time. The emergency room physician had called me to look at X-rays that had been taken of the patient. I read them as negative. A day later, after the patient had been sent home, I received a call that she was in another hospital with a fracture of the cervical spine (neck).

I learned in the following three years of constant haranguing by attorneys from both sides that fear can take over and make life a living hell. It was psychologically devastating to me and my family. Had I gone into the final court room scene with that attitude, it would have scarred me forever and certainly would not have improved my self esteem as the lawyer for the plaintiff sought to discredit all those being sued.

I was amazed and totally excited about the change in my attitude since my Esalen experience. I had no fear or doubt and looked upon the court proceedings as an outside observer might look at it. It was fascinating to observe the seriousness of all concerned and the amount of psychic energy being used by the judge, the jury and both lawyers. I was not even nervous as I took the stand. On the final day as I was going up in the elevator to the court room, a well dressed young lady was the only other occupant. For some reason she told me that she was going to a court room where her husband was going to make a lot of money today and they had planned a grand vacation and purchase of many items that they wanted from winning the case. She did not realize I was one of the defendants, until we got to the court.

I waited, meditating, as the jury left to make its decision in the matter. When they returned, the foreman gave the "not guilty" verdict and it was over. When my lawyer gleefully said, "We won!" I had to ask him what we had won. I had almost let it destroy my life because of the stress. Fortunately, I was able to know that no matter what the verdict was, I had finally approved of myself and no longer needed the approval of others.

AN OBSERVATION ON MEN CHANGING

It became evident on my second trip to the Esalen Institute how many men react and resolve the great metamorphosis of self. My room mate was going through some of the "Finding who I am" stuff and when he thought that he had found it, he called his wife and told her he would not be coming home. Perhaps that was music to her ears, but I perceived it as a negative ending to a positive process for both of them. In another instance, there was a German World Banker employee that traveled that great distance to also find himself. While undergoing his metamorphosis, he notified his business partners and family in Germany that he would not be returning. He stayed at Esalen for some time and then moved to LA. I am not sure if that is gaining freedom but I cannot judge his journey. I can only observe it.

The most often asked question concerning my great change is, "Are you still with your wife?" as if that would not be an option or that one would be expected to leave loved ones, or unloved ones, behind and scurry off to La La land. I might have thought that at times before and during psychotherapy but the desire to share my new found joy with those with whom I had lived somewhat dysfunctionally overcame those leanings. When I accepted that I was the one that needed to change, it was no longer a challenge for me to change others into what I wished them to be. My focus was on helping them on their own journey, to be the best that they could be, without reservation. I did not have to agree with them or particularly like what they seemed to be, but I did love them enough to know they came to live their own lives and not that of another. What a beautifully difficult lesson to learn. And I am still learning it.

16

COMING FULL CIRCLE

THE FINAL CHAPTER

Now, how on Earth can I write a final chapter that will pull together all that I have been trying to say, so that it will make some kind of sense to the reader? I would hope that reading this book will have helped you to see your life in a different way than you have in the past and that it will encourage you to ask and answer your own questions about life.

I am not trying to change anyone other than myself, nor the perception of who I am. I came to Earth to live in this container (that would be the human body) and have had all these awesome experiences. It is a manner of sharing from my own context of life so that all readers may read it from the context of their own lives and have a little Light shined on their own existence.

I have not wanted to offend anyone, to "get back" at anyone, or to blame anyone for who I am or where I am in this Earth life. Some of those whom I have mentioned might take it that way, especially family members who might find it difficult to understand that I love them, just as I love myself. That does not mean that I agree with them in all things or, in some cases, even want to be around them. It is not a judgment of any, since that would just be judging myself.

Perhaps I will write some points, succinctly, in an attempt to shorten what it has taken so long for me to say. I will attempt to do that with the following list of things that I believe are generally applicable to all.

1. We cannot blame anyone for who we are.
2. We cannot change anyone but ourselves.
3. A gift is not ours until we give it away.
4. When we judge others, we are judging ourselves.
5. When we do good to others, we are doing good to ourselves.
6. We are not separate from the Universe.
7. We are not separate from each other.
8. We are not separate from God, Creator, Creation, Light.
9. We are ONE WITH ALL.
10. We cannot love others if we do not love ourselves.
11. We cannot receive love if we do not love ourselves and know that we are worthy of being loved.
12. When I give a gift to someone, I am giving it to myself.
13. When I love someone, I am loving myself.
14. I am the Beloved.
15. You are the Beloved.

and finally....

When it is my turn to be God, I want to make a world that is beautiful with trees, grass, rivers, oceans and wonderful animals and birds and fishes of all kinds. Then, I will make some people or bodies, or containers or whatever you want to call them. These beings will be very intricate and have everything they need to exist already built in.

Then, the spirits that already and have forever existed, will choose the bodies that they want to inhabit while they work out their journeys, or their salvation, as some will undoubtedly call it. There will be total freedom of choice to make whatever decisions and perceptions that they want to make. The energy that they expend in living their Earth lives will be the energy that propels their spiritual evolution which will have an effect on the entire Universe, in a positive way.

And when they think they are in trouble, I will listen to them and remind them that they already have all the power of the Universe at their disposal and just need to remember that. And, the remembering of that is, again, the positive force that will help them spiritually evolve. I will send special souls to them to remind them of how awesome they are and have always been and that they are really ONE with me, so that all that I have, they have.

I won't interfere when they forget who they are or when they forget to take care of the bodies that I have made for them. I won't interfere when they make choices that cause harm to the bodies and emotions of others but will let them work that out themselves, a process which also motors the evolutionary process. I will remind them that they can't do it wrong and to stop worrying about the outcome, which will be what it will be.

I will remind them that I am not going to punish them for the choices that they have made because I gave them that freedom. What kind of a God would I be if I took that back. I will remind them that they are swimming in my Love and it is always there, sustaining them, no matter what they do on Earth.

I will encourage them to love themselves for their Magnificence and to share that love with all others and everything else that I have made. After all, they created what IS with me, since we are and have always been ONE.

Wait a minute. The One that is God now has already done that. How can I top that?

EPILOGUE

FOR LOVERS OF POETRY

I wrote the following poems at various times throughout my life, and have chosen not to include them in the body of the book. I will try to remember why I wrote them and the emotions through which I was going at the time. I always hated it in high school when the teacher would have us read a poem and ask, "What does the poet mean?" Geez! Like the poet may not even have known what they meant. Perhaps it is our "Greater Self" speaking through us in poetry trying to get our attention. You will have to decide.

The first poem sort of reviews all that I have said in the book, if you diligently read between the lines. It seems natural to relate a lot of my life to the drum and drumming. Almost all little children like to drum and dance.

THE OLDE DRUMMER BOY
I've enjoyed the "Little Drummer Boy" music
For many years
It's brought feelings of love and joy
Sometimes tears
I was never quite sure why these many emotions
Visited me
What personal worth they had, if any
I could not see
For after all, a child is a drummer
Quite naturally
Before each has been told what they
"Ought to be."
I lived the life of "Ought to be" for
Three score years and six
Believing to survive this life I must lay down
The drummer's sticks

But, borrowing from Milton's "On His Blindness" to
Escape my strife
"Patience to prevent that murmur soon replies."
I drum to share my joy of life.

 CB80

This next poem is an attempt, and you may think a "poor" one, to be funny in a serious way, whatever that means. Perhaps it is a call to "lighten up."

THE MOUSE IN THE MANGER

We have all heard the story
Of the Christmas birth glory
How in the manger that night
Was the birth of pure Light

But few have been told
Of a story so bold
Of a creature so lowly
Near a newborn so Holy

In the manger of hay
He was swept quite away
When he looked up to see
What brought forth so much glee

So tiny and furry
He had to hurry
To the corner he went
For a night quite well spent

What feelings went through
What great blessing he knew
As he watched the new child
With the hay round him piled

A bright light shone here
From the Holy One near
A warmth through his body
Like a very hot toddy

Who was this creature
Who looked on His feature
Was filled with such bliss
When by mother was kissed

Four legs and a tail
A bit larger than a snail
The manger was a house
For this sweet little mouse.

ೞ೮

*My obviously pregnant daughter-in-law, with
soul inside surrounded by warmth and activity stirred
this next offering on 11-29-1992*

The Earth as a womb, inside out
Activity and heat at the center
Deep earthy noises and redness flowing
Ever out to the numberless movings
Struggling to gain foothold
To stay un-aborted
Trying to avoid the coat hanger of life
Holding the breath from the toxins of air
Ranting and raving, crying for food
Some pre, some post dated birth
But all, yes all of unlimited worth

ೞ೮

*The occasion of the next poem burns deeply
within me even as I type this. It was in honor of a
bright soul in her thirties whose presence was taken
from us at the time of the Murrah Building bombing
took place in Oklahoma City. Susan had been a belly*

*dancer for the Jewels of the Nile and was also an
excellent drummer, who had drummed in my home. She
was truly an inspiration. I was asked by her pastor to
lead a memorial drumming, during which I placed a
very large and special drum that I had made just for
the occasion in the center of the circle.*

THE DRUMMING

Seemed the thing to do, to drum for Susan
To celebrate her life, not her death
When called upon to do this task
With old and trembling hands, I felt unsure

I sought the help of computer Friends
From Coast to Coast they sent their strength
Because of this, I sat a drum quite large
For them to play, along with Susan

Across the drum were two fine mallets
For friendly spirits to wield in her honor
As spirits soared, sounds did come from hearts thru drum
The mallets stayed, unmoved

Then unannounced, two preteen lasses entered the circle
Each took a mallet, circled the drum, and set the beat
My dearest friend, next to me, gently touched and said
"There are your spirits!"
ೞ౮ಀ

*As mentioned in the body of this book, I had a
rather awesome "day vision" during which I was
accepted into the Esselen tribe and given the name of
Littlegull. The "gull" motif obviously relates to my "Big
Bang" experience of re-birth centering on sea gulls.
The "spirit trees" had to be the fantastic giant
Redwoods of California, those gentle giants which kiss
the sky.*

148

FLY WILD

Fly wild, fly wild
My sweet sea gulls
To the Esselen Indian spirits
In the trees
In the trees of red
Of two thousand years
My tribe, my tribe
How I long to be with you
With your simple truths
Your simple pleasures

Fly wild, fly wild
Circle the trees
That hold my brothers
The spirits that give
Me strength to live
And hope that I
Too may find the oneness
With Mother Earth and
Father Sun
How I long to be with you

Mother, father and tiny bird
That my re-birth did make
On those slopes of old
Near boiling bath
My brother surf still calls
My name
As tiny whale plays
Silly game
Littlegull, Littlegull
I am you, I am YOU
෴

*Creede, Colorado was the place mentioned in
the book where my family seemed real to me. This*

poem was written as part of a local artists renderings in the tiny mining town in Southwest Colorado. My father had bought the ancient house in 1942, left it to us, and we modernized it and spend as much time there as possible. Occasionally an eagle will fly overhead and let us know of its presence with its piercing song.

LOOK UP CREEDE

Look up Creede!
To six pines on the hill
Below the yellow pines
South of Isch

Do you see an old house there
Rebuilt and winterized?
Only a picture in 1892
In the history of Creede

Who lived there
In the darkness and cold?
In the fine soot
That choked lungs and clothes?

Did you care about them?
Did they care about you?
Or do you hide in your houses
Trying to keep your pipes from freezing?

I know of one group
Some may recall
A family there
But nowhere else

A place to laugh
Clean fish
Play cards
Sleep well.

The old man, gone now
But spirit remains
He watches you
And loves you

Look up Creede!
What do you see?
I see my father
He was my father there
ଔଚ

The following is an attempt to lighten up and
offer something on the funnier side of life, although
still describing how we repress who we are. So, maybe
it is not so light. Its tough to be a cowboy.

SILLY LITTLE DITTY

A cowboy don't go
To a Shrink, ya know
Because of what his friends might say
It'd frighten all the cowgirls away

But this old rider
Drank too much cider
Decided he needed to see a doc
Before he turned to shattered rock

He rambled in
After a shot of gin
His shoulders in a slouch
To lie down on the healing couch

She looked at him
A sight so grim
She had a doubt, to make an attempt
To help this critter, so unkempt

But she looked "inside"
This redneck hide
For the world had need
Of this kind of breed

So she pushed up her glasses
And remembered her classes
That taught her how to talk and act
And with this cowboy made a wholesome pact

They worked day and night
With many a fight
He fought back with a mighty fuss
She almost gave up on this old cuss

But by her wit
She made him fit
Although his head was a'swimmin
A nice cowboy that was liked by women

୧୫୨୦

*Ouch! I hope this does not drag you down too
far, as it was written in desparate times of
hopelessness and tells of the internal struggles with my
mother and by my mother. Written July 15, 1988.*

STRUGGLES

I love her more in death than life
For her there was naught but strife
From beginning toil till time was gone
The world between us was all wrong

My anger was kept deep inside
And this did make such poor abide
Better said and out with it
Than live in gloomy, worldly pit

I should have fought for that my right
Instead, I lived in constant night
But I see now it is quite true
She also had her fight to do.

Her mother was much like herself
Had selfish heart, no earthly wealth
She struggled for some sign of worth
From end of life since time of birth

Too busy was she with this quest
With spouse or children to do her best
It grows more plain to understand
As life slips by like grains of sand

I will love her and love I should
For one I have not understood
I see she had no time for me
So deep in struggle of life was she
ᑲᕒᑯ

*I love the concept and the writings of Chief
Seattle about the "Web of Life" which occasioned this
next poem. An attempt to say what I consider that web
to be. Written on April 13, 1993.*

THE WEB-OF-LIFE

The poets
At least the ones I read
Have many ways
To tell of their need
Some despondent
Over life poorly done
Others with a glimpse
Of life after this one

I take from each
The ingredients I choose
Blend them together
But gently, not to bruise

I roll them around
In my Inner Man's mouth
Till smooth and quite tasty
To smother the drought

Like the spider I know
I turn it to silk
And add my own web
To others of like ilk

To the giant Web-Of-Life
Unlimited by space
I add my small web
And join in the race

But, small as it is
It has an effect
On others connected
And on me, I suspect

Let the energies flow
Throughout the Web's length
So others may know
The source of life's strength

An eyebrow is raised
Can he really be serious
And he glibly replies
God still works mysterious

ෆ෨

*I hope the following is self explanatory. It was
written a year after the beginning of my awakening.*

154

ON REACHING 63

And I am sixty-three
The major part of me
Well past
But the best
Part of me
Still to come
In ALL its glory
And the people said
"AMEN"
଼ଃ଼

*Oh My! The feelings that I get when I read this
one. I did not know at the time but it is in honor of one
whom I consider the World's best Family Doctor. He
helped me live, but himself he could not help. I honor
his journey. He was in the hospital for a short time and
this was my way of saying "Bob. I love you." Written
Oct 9, 1991.*

To: Dr. Bob Daniels in the hospital

THE UNPOEM

I've heard you have plenty of flowers
To while away the hours
So I thought a little poem
Would not cause any hoem. (Harm doesn't rhyme)

The flowers you have to smell
Which may help make you well
You only have to read a poem
To make you laugh and kill a goem (germ doesn't rhyme either)

You know that you're my only Doc
So be real strong and like a rock (Hey. That rhymes)
Get well quick, come back real soon
And leave that dreary hospital roon (room doesn't rhyme either)
଼ଃ଼

As you can see, the next was in the dark days while trying to make acceptable sense out of life. The words expressed that which the poet did not understand. And, in the end, reverting to something outside of self as the only hope. Written on Aug. 28, 1985.

WHAT AGE THE SPIRIT

What age is the spirit within this hulk
IS it measured by sight. Is it measured by bulk
Does the receding pate, the grayness of hair
Give a true indication of what really is there

The baby, the child, adolescent and all
Seek to break out if someone would call
Are laughter and joy and sadness and coy
And all other attributes of a little boy

To remain prisoner for evermore
In this shabby old frame that creaks cross the floor
Is there some other form this spirit could take
That doesn't lie sleeping but fully awake

Compassionate, caring, ready to be
Whatever is needed for all to see
What a terrible task to put in short verse
To be quiet or scream out, whichever is worse

Eventually though, when man turns to dust
The spirit lives on, safe in God's trust
ଊଞ

Tell me what you think the next poem means, not to the poet, but to you the reader.

FEELINGS

Feelings surging to be released
As lava erupts from a volcano
Good feelings that heal and
Enhance those that it touches.
Feelings that encompass and warm
And make everything all better.
Sad that these feelings cannot
Be expressed for there are many
Standing in line for the expression.

Must these beautiful energies
Be forever stilled in this life
Or is there hope of release in
The next existence?
This my comfort, that the beauty
Of sharing will find a sharer
Now, or then
To be open, not to oppress
Letting it flow as the friction
Allows the beginning of this
New life form, dreamed of
But, so far, un-experienced.

০৩৪০

While I do not like to think of "regrets," this expresses a bent to hold on to the old ways. The occasion was after the bombing in Oklahoma City and Babatunde Olatunji called me at 1:00 AM and asked me to get a committee together and plan on his coming to Oklahoma City to do a healing drumming. He would bring many drummers with him and it would all be free. We would be joined by drummers around the World. After a few telephone calls, the "powers that be" were put in touch with Baba. Baba was not one for paperwork, nor am I and was not keen on having to write reams of justification for this and that. Needless

to say, he was not asked to come, some fearing a
security problem with drummers drumming all night,
or so they said. Oklahoma never had the honor of
Baba's sharing of his Universal Love. It would have
brought healing like Oklahoma has never seen.

TO THOSE HURTING IN OKLAHOMA

(after the Murrah Building bombing)

The spirit moved to such degree
And stirred the hearts of all who heard
To drum to heal the pain that lay
And feelings deep that words can't say

The heart of Baba was want to try
To come to this scarred place of woe
To drum the healing sound of life
And rid the place of ancient foe

For several days the stream ran fast
There looked no end to this rapid pace
But "Reason" raised it's ugly head
And cast the anchor on this race

"Twas not my loss" I told my heart
My energies had spoken true
The Shaft of Practicality
Has pierced the hearts of You

ଓ୫୦

I have a sneaky feeling that you will quickly
sense that I was not in a good place when the next
poem was written. I don't even know why I wrote it, but
it seemed to be necessary at the time. I think it could
also be called "Caught in Chaos" and you will again
notice my only "out" was to turn to something "out
there." Written on Oct 8, 1985.

CONSTERNATION

In the middle of a piddle
In the middle of a puddle
Nothing seems to come together
Everything just seems a muddle

In the middle of a huddle
All the sounds my mind befuddle
Nothing seems to come together
All my thoughts the sounds do scuttle

In the middle of a hassle
Every day becomes a frazzle
Nothing seems to come together
My existence weak as a tassal

In the middle of my castle
All my mind is like a vassal
Nothing seems to come together
Life's insistent foes I wrestle

Do not be discontented
All the world you have resented
Everything will come together
If you only have repented.

03800

Oh Wow! Boy. Do I remember this one.
Around the time I attempted to enter the spirit world. It
is actually a note that I wrote to my psychotherapist.
Think I was depressed?

JUNE 11, 1988 A NOTE TO HIS THERAPIST

He was born to be a child of despair
A beast without a beauty
A Cyrano without a Roxanne
An arrow without a target

A tide going out but never coming in
A love without a lover
A dancer without a partner

A beating heart without blood
A gift with no place to go
A river without water
A life without a purpose

Who will help
Who will call
Who will care
Who will see

They came
They knocked
They opened the door
No one was there

My heart cried out for help and all I got was a busy signal
Francis, between now and Thursday, we need to think of a
good reason for me to keep on living.

ଷ୍ଠେ

*This is the first of two similar poems with only
tiny differences. While I looked forward to Christmas
as a child, I found myself to be very sad when it arrived
and the more presents I got, the sadder I became. It is
thought by some psychotheraists that the reason so
many are depressed at Christmas is not that they do
not get what they think they want, but don't think they
deserve what they get. This is all in the subconscious
and not to be explained in a sentence or two. But, it
does explain where the poet thought he was on June
27, 1994.*

IN SEARCH OF CHRISTMAS I

Too many times I've heard the tale
Of the Christmas downer
I knew quite well of the dread
This hapless day could bring
"Was only me, no other felt this way"
I would say to the young heart that felt no worth
And gifts could only bring shame and guilt
T'was easy to give but never quite enough. I
Thought to "pay my dues" and gain a nod
A nod from whom?
Went on this way for 62 years till the Fates would
Bring a wingless Angel to be my guide
To see the heart and mind inside were mine
To mold and shape
Three other Angels came along, Gloria with her
Revolution, Shirley with her Dance, and , yes
Even Rosanne who wields her hammer with rusty
Truth, woke up the "sleeper."
Now Christmas is welcome within my soul
As I receive with open arms, those shared emotions
That others want to heap on me, this self that once
Was bathed in guilt, now gilded with Self Esteem,
Peace of mind, Contentment, yes
The Gift by Spirit given
Christmas Found
ෆ෨ං

*A little different "take" on the guilts of
Christmas on June 27, 1994.*

IN SEARCH OF CHRISTMAS II

Black snow fell each Christmas
Midst all the bustle,
Feigned joy of others
There was no joy for me.
Each gift like a barbed hook
Fastened itself to me
And built guilt upon guilt until
I cried for an end to it.
"Nothing hath befallen you
That is not common to all"
Kept ringing in my soul but
Surely there must be joy for others
Or were all playing the game well?
God sent a wingless Angel
That guided me from Hell
And took me to that Inner Man
That He had made so well
A child of beauty, forever there
Waiting to take my hand in search
Of peace of mind, contentment, joy
All there, just waiting to be owned
Three other Angels, without wings
Were sent to guide my path
Gloria, with her "Revolution,"
Shirley, with her "Dance,"
And, even Roseanne, whose
Blacksmith blows of rusty truth
Helped forge esteem of self
A rebirth of sorts, an awakening perhaps,
That changed the colors of Christmas
The snow falls white and coats my soul
That now can take with joy
The gifts to be received.
Christmas found!

03⬥80

*See if you can make any sense of this. I can,
sometimes.*

A SILLY THING

You can't pour water on the bottom of a cup
It'll spill right off and fill the table up
It must be upright if its gonna hold a thing
You can have a choice of a puddle or a spring

Life's like that as you wander down the way
You must decide if you wanna work or play
You can have a ball and from the carnal sup
But you can't pour water on the bottom of a cup.

ଓଃ୭

*This poem was inspired while watching our
very smart Siamese cat trying to open a door to the
outside. There were keys hanging from the keyhole and
Fooh Puma had managed to stretch his long and lyth
body enough to touch the keys and then try to turn the
door knob as he had seen us do. He was also very good
at opening kitchen drawers, even those taped shut to
keep him out. Written Sept 17, 1985.*

THUMB CAT

I have often thought, if I had a thumb
What a wonderful world this could be
And my feline friends would not think me dumb
If I could do more than just climb a tree

If I had a thumb, I could turn the key
And then turn the knob that opens the door
And this would truly excite even me
To hurry outside, the world to explore

If I had a thumb, the pantry door I'd loose
And forthwith hurry in to look
For now there would be no more to the truce
And I could eat every thing that I took

If I had a thumb, I would take all the cans
To the can opener they would go
For no longer would this domain be the man's
For want of a thumb or a toe.

If I had a thumb, I would open the box
That contains all the needles and thread
I would spread them all over as sly as a fox
And then hide them under the bed

If I had a thumb, I would look pretty silly
While trying to do things I just shouldn't
Running around like a cat willy nilly
To change this much I just couldn't
ଓ৪০

If you don't understand this, you need to stop
reading my poetry. Written Jan 29, 1988.

SURRENDER

Where do you go to surrender?
Where do you go to give up?
I'm tired of the great conflagration
I feel like a clown and a pup

I've given it all that I can
I thought I had done it correctly
Evidently I have been mistaken
If you look at it circumspectly

Damned if you're too kindhearted
Damned if you over express
So I still have the same old problems
How do I get out of this mess?

ᬓᬰᬑ

Have you ever wanted to write someone and
really tell them off? Me to, and that is the reason for
writing the following poem.

THE LETTER I ALMOST MAILED

Have you ever said
I wrote this letter from deepest heart
But afraid to mail and tore it apart
I'm sure I'm not the only one
That's done this deed while on the run
To the minister at church
Who began to delve
Into personal things you wish he'd shelve
To the minister of music
Who doesn't understand
That I have the best voice in the land
To the Council of a local town
Who knows very little when you're around
To the baseball coach of your oldest son
This is serious business and not for fun
To your bright child's teacher
If she only knew.
What great things your child can do
To the physician, your money he took
Why, you could have done that right out of a book
To the lawyer in politics
What does he know
Only to raise taxes, the old so and so
And last to the President
Who stands on the brink

If he listens to me, I'll tell him what to think
What a fine world it would turn out to be
If they would all only listen to little ol' me.

ꝏ

*Oh boy! Be careful when you call Death. What
is the old saying "Be careful what you ask for?" I
almost got it while trying to run my car into a highway
concrete abuttment but "chickened out" at the last
moment. Thank you Mr. Chicken.*

CALLING DEATH (ABOUT 1985)

Come sweet death and release
Me from this form I fear so much
I yearn for that eternal peace
So come with sickle this body touch

I see that when still a child
A man within this frame was locked
Then when a man with thoughts so wild
A child entrapped, escape was blocked

No time is there to find a cause
Nor is there time to find a cure
The past reflection takes quite a pause
The end of time comes very sure

Too late to cry out or ask
"What age the spirit within this hulk?"
Or to awake and throw off the mask
Whether measured by sight or by bulk

Just to exist and play the game
Is all that's left for me to do
Forget the joy and be quite lame
Hasten the day all will be through.

ꝏ

*I was just messing around when I wrote the
following as I was remembering some of my class
mates at different sessions at the Esalen Institute on
Big Sur in California. A sort of weird thing to do and
have not done since.*

SOME THOUGHTS ABOUT FELLOW SELF ESTEEM CLASS MEMBERS

You touched me
With your anger
Repressed, but not always

You touched me
With your loneliness
But pulled back when I approached

What lovely angry fires
Belched forth when you
Danced wildly to Enigma

How proud of you I was
When you made life decisions
And suffered with your mate

You were wed
As never before
With the Jewishness of the group

Proud
So serene
You enveloped me

A beauty.
Of other nature
I could have loved you

Cold
A Canadian heart
Warming only little

Strong appearance
Danger, danger
This one could explode

A helper
Burned out
Is there no one to help him?

The mouth
Graying
Cannot help for the noise

A couple
A chance
Red hair has doubts

Hollywood
Glitter
Can't get out

The leader
The child
Man's body

ଔଓ

*Oh yes! This brings back such pleasant
memories. There were two giant Monterey Pine trees, a
few feet apart on a cliff overlooking a beautiful stream
at Esalen. It became a routine as I made my "magic"
walk each morning to situate myself between them, just
being able to place the palms of my hands, one on each
tree. I could feel the pulse of their heart beat. Written
July 21, 1993.*

168

COMMUNION

Two stately cedars side by side
Did share the space by Big Sur's tide
Their heads were thrust into the sky
Far from my view as I passed by

When spirit calls I cannot resist
To stop and stare through gentle mist
They pull me near deep feelings rise
To commune with them, these giants of sky's

I plant my feet half way between
And stretch my arms on both to lean
I wait for signs I have not known
But I am free these signs to own

Soon, from the bowels of Mother Earth
Come waves of love of greater worth
They send through me, free man so young
Wisdom of ages in songs they sung

I stood transfixed unable to move
As if to them my worth to prove
I am undone, I am overcome
And yet there was much more for this one

My quaking hands still on their skin
Began to move and go within
These giant's of mine who hold the essence
Of long gone Esalen's, I feel their presence

My hands go deep, their hearts I feel
We are now one, my mind doth reel
I must come back or ever stay
In this blessed state, the spirit way

I did recoil and pull away
Fearful was I of this mind play
My soul cries out for more of this
Now that I know of utter bliss

ᭅᬫᭀ

*This is the story of my "firstborn," a little
drum that I made and still have. It was an awesome
experience and ended in a childlike glee as it spoke to
me upon being finished. It still speaks. The thought
occurred as I was watching the life of Elizabeth
Bishop, a poet, that she was so good at relating her
feelings in terms of her environment.*

THE DRUM (NUMERO UNO)

Is this what poetry is
I had to ask
Or is a poet and the poetry
Forever to escape explanation?

My life of late has been a race
More or less
To "finish" my drum
Or is a drum ever finished?

It started with the wood, of course
Bought with the purpose in mind of
Not spending too much since I had
Never built a drum before.

I was excited to begin but it was hard
To use materials of great worth that
Cost little, and an uncomfortable feeling
Accompanied this attempt.

How can one build a cheap masterpiece?
I think it now but was careful to
Avoid this thought at the
Creation

Pine is fine. It is alive with softness
And smell
Easy to shape or replace if
A mistake is made

The skeleton was so easy
Thirty minutes to cut and glue
And the basic life was there
Without undue notice

The boards were too heavy and
Would dull the sound that would ensue
If left that way to receive
The pounding of life to come

Gentle thinning until
The thickness was reached
To vibrate the message
Of each blow to optimum

Far from done
The work to come
To turn this bowl into
A drum

Hard metal rings
Shaped by hand
The ends held fast
By bolt from Zeus

The head by way
Of a goat did come
To make the sound
Of this first drum

Plain at first
Then painted white
But still not seen
For what it was

A mixture of good and evil
By spirals white and black
Brought no more joy
Than the others

The rulers cast off
A free hand paints
The colors of life
Green, yellow, red & black

The work sprang forth
With life anew
Joy and sadness
And mind set free

 og80